GOD'S DESIGN FOR RELATIONSHIPS

LEE E. EDDY

ISBN 978-1-64114-399-8 (paperback)
ISBN 978-1-64114-400-1 (digital)

Christian Faith Publishing, Inc.
832 Park Avenue
Meadville, PA 16335
www.christianfaithpublishing.com

Unless otherwise noted, all Scripture quotations are taken from the Literal Translation of the Holy Bible, third edition, copyright 1997. Used by permission of the copyright holder, Jay P. Green, Sr.

Printed in the United States of America

CONTENTS

DEDICATION

My incredible wife, Roxanne, has been my partner, my critic, my sounding board, the one who has stood with me through all the circumstances in life that taught me about relationships, and the one who has loved me through it all. Between you and Jesus, I am above all men most blessed.

ACKNOWLEDGEMENTS

Thanks to all who patiently walked with me and believed in what Jesus was doing in my life. Thanks to Bruce and Nancy for your editing and input. Thanks to Jesus for putting up with me in all the relationship missteps. No one learns this with clean hands. I am so grateful.

INTRODUCTION

"Come down and teach on relationships."

That was the email request I received while my family and I were missionaries in Russia.

The Youth With A Mission (YWAM) base in the southern part of Russia had written to request that I come and teach the Discipleship Training School. The students needed to know how to survive ministry out in the world for the first time.

"That is a little vague," I wrote back. "What relationships do you want me to teach about?"

"All."

Imagine trying to prepare teaching for a week-long class which included all forms of relationships. What I found out later was that they wanted teachings on how to handle the opposite sex. Too late. I had already developed a firm understanding on all relationships.

What transpired next was beyond my highest expectations. I found out that Christians have very little understanding of what the Bible says about conducting relationships. We are often just as susceptible as the world about how to treat our fellow man and we will fight to the end to defend our position regardless how much damage it causes.

As I was teaching this in various places, people would come up to me and thank me for helping them understand for the first time how they are to interact with others in their lives.

I also had many people try to pick a fight with me! They didn't like me meddling in their spats and telling them how they should have responded. They felt I made them look foolish.

The reality is this: it isn't easy to live like the Lord tells us to live. The very fabric of our Christianity is shown by the way we treat one another. When we don't live correctly, it shows and we look foolish. It takes real courage to humble ourselves and respond the way God would have us respond.

Relationships form the very center of our lives. How we get along with people is of far greater importance than we think. Other people give us insight into different perspectives. We are very concerned with how people treat us but are not often that concerned with how we treat others. The Golden Rule, "Do unto others as you would have them do unto you" sounds good. It just isn't all that easy to do, nor does it feel good to us. We want to treat others a lot worse than how we want them to treat us.

Our human interaction is the focal point of whether we are fulfilled in life or not. Damaged relationships shape the way we live and how we react when others touch our lives. How are we supposed to do things? If we could only learn how to handle the relationships in our lives, wouldn't life be a lot easier? Shouldn't we be able to see Christ work through us in every situation we encounter? The answer to this last question is a resounding "Yes!"

That is what this book is all about. My goal is to give you all that you will need to respond in relationships correctly. The Bible has a lot to say about how we are to treat people and how we should relate to them. There is a lot to say on each subject, but I have tried to slim it down to the essentials. Each chapter is tied in to the others. This is a package deal. Soon the principles you see in one chapter will show up as pertinent building blocks in each new area.

Welcome to the great adventure: living on this planet with the six billion other people. Seems like a good idea to learn how to relate to them, doesn't it?

CHAPTER ONE

HOW TO SEE YOURSELF

If a person doesn't know how to see himself correctly, he will never learn how to see other people correctly. If I have a skewed view of myself, I will act in ways detrimental to myself and others.

This concept can get very complex. As you can see in figure one on page 14, my view of myself in the natural realm alone gets very complicated.

First of all, my father sees me as a son. When I am with him, I act like a son to him. I treat him with respect and honor him, even though we joke around a lot. I am still his son, no matter how old I am or what else is true about me.

My brother, however, sees me as a brother with all the disrespect that being siblings might generate. We have a good relationship, but we treat each other as if we were brothers because we are. I don't treat anyone like I treat him because he is the only brother I have. We are very comfortable with those parameters.

Then along comes my son. He sees me as his father and I respond in that manner. I treat him according to what this relationship requires. I am in a leadership role and have a wonderful relationship with him. We have a wonderful time together. We know our positions and live that way.

On the other hand, my wife has a unique way of seeing me. She and I have entered into a marriage covenant together and that qualifies everything. I am her husband only. I am not in the role of husband to anyone else on the planet (Praise God!). Our views of each other and the positions we hold are very strong and not to be discounted.

Now, to really make things interesting, let's throw in a very different relationship—friendship. My friend sees me as a friend and I see myself as a friend. We have a great time and love to hang around with each other. We prefer to be with each other and have many adventures. I am not a son, brother, father, or husband to him. I act completely different when I am around him than anyone else.

This all makes me very complex. I am a son, brother, father, husband, and friend. But that isn't all I am. I am also the pastor of a church and have many other complex relationships. I am in spiritual authority and yet submitted to higher authority. I can be a friend and yet in an instant be the one in charge. I can flop back and forth. I can be the pastor overseeing what happens in the church service and still be totally submitted to the worship leader as the bass player in his band.

If at any time I act differently than the position I am truly in, I can hurt people, mess up an entire function at the church, or even cause damage that may take months to bring about reconciliation. All that pressure is on me because people are tender because of the pain they have received in relationships.

We are now going to look at several "hats" we all wear as Christians. Each hat of relationship we wear is true, but each one has with it both responsibilities and benefits. We can see each one in a good way or in a bad way. We can use these hats to help people or hurt people. It is very important that we see them for what they truly are based upon the scripture that gives us the insight.

The Father

The Father God of the universe sees me as His son. I see myself as the son of the Most High God. I didn't always see myself that way. I saw the Father as a source of wrath and condemnation. Imagine my surprise and wonder when I was praying one day and I saw something I had never seen before. I saw two doors that were at least twenty feet tall opening by themselves. Inside was a crowd that couldn't be counted and a red carpet that stretched from the door into the center of the room. I started running down that carpet with an intense desire to go all the way. I saw the Father sitting on a throne with everyone watching Him and intently listening to everything He said. As I ran toward Him, everyone got quiet. They were smiling. The Father saw me coming and sat there beaming at me. I realized I was just a child and I ran up and climbed on His lap. He was huge and just enveloped me in His arms. I was welcome on the lap of the King and all business stopped as I was welcomed onto His lap. It was the first time I had seen myself as the son of the Most High God. All I could do was weep in joy. I have never lost that view. Having this view is both very good and very bad. Why is that? Let's look at the scripture.

Romans 8:12-16

So, then, brothers, we are debtors, not to the flesh, to live according to flesh, for if you live according to flesh, you are going to die. But if by the Spirit you put to death the practices of the body, you will live. For as many as are led by the Spirit of God, these are sons of God. For you did not receive a spirit of slavery again to fear; but you received a Spirit of adoption by which we cry, Abba! Father! The Spirit Himself witnesses with our spirit that we are children of God.

We received a Spirit of Adoption! By that Spirit we cry out to the Father the very familiar term, "daddy." The Holy Spirit of God tells us that we are the very children of God. What a wonderful thing that God has done in our lives to actually give us birth into His family. When we were born again, we received exactly that new birth into a new family that just happens to have the God of the Universe as the Father! We are His children and have all the benefits of that relationship. This is totally true and not to be denied. This also produces a few problems, however.

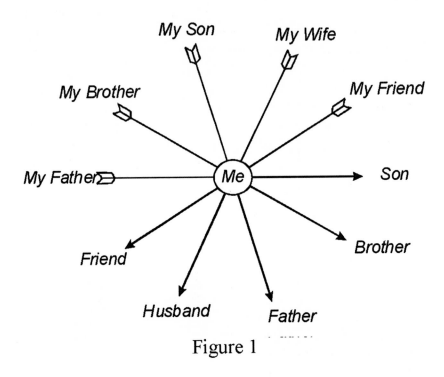

Figure 1

If we didn't have a good relationship with our earthly father, we will probably impose those same problems on our Heavenly Father. So many see God as someone who is just waiting to strike them in His wrath, or even mess them up like a mean little kid messes with ants with his magnifying glass. That is how I used to think about Him even though I had a good relationship with my dad. It was how I was taught about the Father that messed me up. Some may think He is an absentee father or a distant, unfeeling one. Many people have no idea what a good relationship with a male figure looks like and that makes it very hard to figure out how to relate to Father God. If their earthly father shamed them, they figure their Heavenly one will too. If you can't please one, you can't please the other.

All that must be done away with. The Heavenly Father wants us to see what a perfect father is supposed to look like. He has so much more in store for us than we have ever allowed ourselves to see, but the revelation of it must be done His way and in His timing.

Galatians 3:26

For you are all sons of God through faith in Christ Jesus.

It is by faith that we get to become the sons of God. Faith is trust in a relationship, trusting a person. It is in our relationship with the Lord that we have the faith to become the sons of God. There is no difference between faith and trust. Faith isn't some kind of new age mystery force. It is only the words we have heard from Him personally that give us faith and the great power that comes with it. We have to hear the promise before we can believe in it. Otherwise it becomes a religious teaching instead of a relationship with Him. The promise manifests when I approach Him and listen, trusting in the relationship. This word shows us that He fulfills His promises.

John 1:12-13

But as many as received Him, to them He gave authority to become children of God, to the ones believing into His name, who were born not of blood, nor of the will of the flesh, nor of the will of man, but were born of God.

We have been given the authority to become the children of God by believing into His name. We were once outside His name. Once we died to ourselves and believed into the new name, we entered into our new family. It was the will of the Father to give me that salvation and to bring me into His family. He chose me and wanted me. The same is true for you. You are so greatly loved and favored by this new Father you have.

1 John 3:1-2

See what manner of love the Father has given us, that we may be called children of God. For this reason, the world does not know us, because it did not know Him. Beloved, now we are the children of God, and it was not yet revealed what we shall be. But we know that if He is revealed, we shall be like Him, because we shall see Him as He is.

Everything is completely based on how much He loves us. He loves us in the way a father should love us. We now have the opportunity to have what we have never had before. We can have the father relationship that our souls have cried out for all our lives.

That said, there is something else that must be stated. Many preachers and teachers have promoted how much we should see ourselves as the sons of God. They teach many things about the Father heart of God and that we should stand in the relationship we have in that capacity. They are not wrong. The outcome has often resulted in a major problem.

So many Christians have seen themselves exclusively as the sons of God to the extent that they lord it over other people and have become puffed up and obnoxious. Their pride has caused so much damage that those who don't have this revelation are beaten down and classified as second-class by themselves or others. This is the greatest danger. When we relate to others, we need to see ourselves correctly. When I am in the presence of the Father, then I can see myself as the son. It isn't something to use for my soulish benefit, however.

To see myself as the son is very good, but I need to realize that I don't have that position to coerce the Father into doing what I want Him to do. It isn't a position of pressure to apply to the throne. As a son, I must have the attitude of humility and respect. I must walk in it as a relationship with Him and know the extent of His love for me.

This isn't about anyone else, it is about how the Father and I relate. I can't use it over anyone else because they are also sons of God and I must respect that in them also. We are all equal in the sight of God; therefore, no favorites. The view of myself as a son should produce in me the desire to help my brothers and sisters rather than looking down on them.

The view of the Father to see me as a son is His point of view. I should bask in it and receive it with all the humility that grace should elicit in me. I have been given a huge gift and massive responsibility to walk in it. What should my attitude be?

Jesus

My relationship with Jesus is different than my relationship with the Father. How does He see me? He is my Savior, Lord, and King. That is my view of Him, but how does He see me?

It is our relationship with Jesus that brings God to the natural man. He became a man so that we could have personal relationship with the God of the universe. He purchased our lives and, therefore, all that we are or ever will be. Our response to Him is to be one of submission and worship. We shouldn't be flippant or overly casual in His presence.

But we are also free to say to Him anything that is on our hearts. He already knows and is very pleased with openness and honesty. He cares for us and what is happening in our lives matters to Him.

1 Peter 5:6-7

Then be humbled under the mighty hand of God, that He may exalt you in time; 'casting all your anxiety onto Him,' because it matters to Him concerning you.

Having His concern as part of our lives is amazing. He really cares what is going on with us. He is actively involved in every aspect of our lives and is concerned which way we are going.

How does He see us? Let's look at what the scripture says regarding this.

Romans 8:16-17

The Spirit Himself witnesses with our spirit that we are children of God. And if children, also heirs; truly heirs of God, and joint-heirs of Christ, if indeed we suffer together, that we may also be glorified together.

The Spirit witnesses with our spirit that we are the children of the Father. Since we are His children, we are also heirs; joint heirs with Jesus. Jesus sees us as the ones who are inheriting what the Father has for us.

Jesus is the firstborn among many brothers (Romans 8:29) so that gives Him a double portion, the law designates. But that just means that He is the one responsible to look over the dispersing of the inheritance among all the other children. Jesus is working hard to make sure we get all that is coming to us from the Father. The only thing that stops that entire process is our not receiving it or not being in the position to receive.

As a loving big brother/executor, He is making sure we don't get what will be harmful to us, but all the things that we are able to receive. Timing is very important and so is our walk with Him in determining our ability to receive.

Faith is not some kind of mystical power that we have inherently. It is trust in a person, listening to personal promises and resting on what was said. Faith comes by hearing the exact, specifically spoken word from God. We can believe what He speaks to us personally. When we have trust in Him, then He can bring to us what is needed in our lives. When we don't receive, it is because we are not in the position of receiving. We ask amiss or want to spend what we get on our own lusts (James 4:2-3). God is too good of an administrator to allow us to blow our inheritance. He wants us to be good sons who know the Father's business and are going about doing it.

Galatians 4:1-7

But I say, Over so long a time the heir is an infant, he being lord of all, does not differ from a slave, but is under guardians and housemasters until the term set before by the father. So we also, when we were infants, we were under the elements of the world, being enslaved. But when the fullness of the time came, God sent forth His Son, having come into being out of a woman, having come under Law, that He might redeem the ones under Law, that we might receive the adoption of sons. And because you are sons, God sent forth the Spirit of His Son into your hearts, crying, Abba! Father! So that you no more are a slave, but a son, and if a son, also an heir of God through Christ.

In our immaturity, we are treated as if we aren't inheriting everything. We have it all legally, but aren't given everything until we can handle it responsibly. Even then, we have problems because of errors in how we believe. We aren't really trustworthy in certain areas of our lives. Anything that we don't have access to causes us to seek the Father about it. That is when He can convict us of the bad ways of thinking and straighten us out. Then we are able to receive things that we weren't able to inherit before.

The good news is that we've been given the Spirit of Adoption so that we have assurance of our relationship with the Father. We have that assurance that He has our care in mind and is wanting to do what is best in our lives. Praise God we can mature in Him and gain access to more of what the Father has for us.

Jesus doesn't see us as slaves or robots that have no input into the relationship. He wants to have intimacy with us in every way. It is the same way we want to have intimacy with our children. It is always fascinating to watch people while they hold a six-month-old baby. They talk to him, make faces and noises, and expect to have an interaction. They try to get the baby to acknowledge them and respond to what they are doing. But that baby won't respond fully because of his immaturity.

It is a lot like that with the Father. He wants more intimacy than we do. He wants to interact with us on much higher levels than we have ever even dreamed about. It is beyond our comprehension.

No matter what our maturity level is, Jesus still sees us as co-heirs to the Father. Jesus is actively trying to show us everything we could possibly need to live as He did on the earth. We are not slaves, but brothers who are working on the same goals, and we have the same purpose and destiny. We are included in the work of the Father here, and what privilege we have been given to be co-heirs with Christ, doing the work of the eternal Kingdom of God. With that as a starting point, we can go even deeper, as it says in His Word.

John 15:13-15

Greater love than this has no one, that anyone should lay down his soul for his friends. You are My friends if you do whatever I command you. I no longer call you slaves, for the slave does not know what his lord does. But I called you friends, because all things which I heard from My Father I made known to you.

He sees us as His friends. But what exactly is it that Jesus is saying to us here? In this passage, He isn't referring to someone who is just a close acquaintance. The term He used for friend is referring to a "covenant friend," and that changes everything.

Our society doesn't understand the depth of covenant since we don't have anything like it in our culture or even collective memory. The closest we have is a contract and there is a major difference between a covenant and a contract.

A contract is dependent upon the actions of the other party. If either party of the contract doesn't fulfill what they said they would do, the other party isn't liable for their part of the contract. If I hired you to paint my house and you didn't paint it, you can't come to me for the money I said I would pay you. However, if you did paint my house and I didn't pay you according to the contract, you could go to the courts and force me to pay.

A covenant is another matter altogether. The relationship of the two parties is based on the commitment each party brings to the covenant. Neither one can complain about the actions of the other party. Each must fulfill their commitment no matter what the other is doing. If the other party isn't doing what they said they would do, it doesn't matter.

This is what makes dealing with marriage a more serious issue then most think it is. Marriage is a covenant. Divorce isn't allowed because of the actions of the other party. The only thing I am bringing to this relationship is the commitment I made; ("Till death do us part") and it doesn't matter what my spouse does or doesn't do. Covenant always shows the depth of love for the other person. I live for my spouse and my spouse lives for me. If there were more commitment in marriages instead of revenge for wrongs done, we would see a lot stronger marriages and a lot fewer children damaged by divorce.

In this passage in John, Jesus is showing us the commitment of covenant. He showed us what greater love is. (I will explain that further in the next chapter.) But more importantly, He showed that if we truly loved Him, we would do what He commanded. We have a huge commitment to the greater scheme of things than just our desire for our own benefit.

He said that He called us friends and no longer slaves. The nation of Israel gave up their relationship with the Lord when they told Moses to speak to God for them and not let Him talk to them directly (Ex. 20:19). That caused them to obey God out of duty and not by relationship. They were nothing short of mere slaves. But then Jesus came and with Him came the restoring of covenant and relationship. He no longer calls us slaves, rather those who have a deep and abiding relationship with Him in covenant. He is so close to us that He is sharing with us everything that the Father is doing. That shows His commitment to us and His reliance on us as individuals to carry out His calling and the purpose of the Father. What a wonderful privilege we have been given.

When I first started doing one-on-one ministry, I discovered something that has been amazing to me ever since. When I talk to Jesus about the person sitting in front of me, He personally comes and speaks to them and me. He isn't lording anything over us, even though He is Lord. He is there as a loving friend and a brother to bring the freedom that is so needed into people's lives. This tender relationship with Him is so practical it is hard to explain or even comprehend. Jesus personally comes to us and talks to us, making the lies we have believed run away and not affect us any longer. It is a highly intimate and tender love that He displays on a continual basis. Lives are changed.

I believe that we have a calling and purpose that is higher than anyone in history. We are those who live this life by the Spirit of God. We have a covenant with the Lord God through Jesus Christ. In that covenant, we have access to all that God is and all He had made us to be. When we come before Him, it is without groveling or cringing. We have direct access to His very throne by the covenant love of the Lord Jesus Christ.

Jesus sees us as those covenant friends that are closer than brothers. We are His co-heirs and then, even more than that, we are in covenant with Him and the Father. They see us as much more than we see ourselves. We are still trying to get God to do what we want instead of submitting to Him and doing what He wants. When we submit to Him, we will be fulfilled in our lives instead of doing all the things that don't fulfill us and take all our energy. Our selfishness drains all our power and ruins our purpose in life.

Look at this passage. It tells us the plan of God and the position we have in Him.

Romans 8:28-29

But we know that to the ones loving God all things work together for good, to those being called accord-

ing to purpose; because whom He foreknew, He also predestinated to be conformed to the image of His Son, for Him to be the First-born among many brothers.

Only the things done by those who are fulfilling the purpose of God have everything in their life work together for good. When we live His purpose, then we are walking His plan. He has determined that those who have faith in God will walk a certain path. He drew up that path a long time ago and then told us to choose. He foreknew the path. Whoever chooses to walk that path is walking in the plan to be conformed to the image of Jesus Christ. When we do that, we are acting like the brothers of the family. We are all working together in the "family business" with our Father. We are then fulfilling our destiny and the fulfillment is very satisfying. Who else can make that claim?

Seeing ourselves as the brother of Jesus, His co-heir, and His covenant friend is accurate. But it is beyond our ability to understand completely. But in reality, that is how He sees us. And again it isn't for us to lord it over anyone else. It really should humble us.

Holy Spirit

Of course, we can't leave the Holy Spirit out of this. He is the part of the Trinity who lives in us and is working with us on a very tight scale.

The Trinity cannot be separated. They can be seen differently, but in reality, they are one. However, we can see the differences in the scripture. The function of the Holy Spirit is the main connection between God and man.

In the passage above (Romans 8:29), the purpose of the Holy Spirit can be seen and that is to conform us to the image of Jesus Christ. He convicts us of all the areas where we don't conform to Jesus. He affirms us in areas where we have been changed and are walking in Him. He gently guides us and speaks to us in so many ways. He gives us understanding. He empowers us to do what we have been commanded to do. He comforts us in the middle of our troubles. He broods over us to bring us into the very place we have been destined to be. He opens our hearts and eyes.

But how does He actually see us? It seems to me that seeing us from His vantage point would be very insightful and beneficial.

2 Corinthians 3:17-18

And the Lord is the Spirit; and where the Spirit of the Lord is, there is freedom. But we all with our face having been unveiled, having beheld the glory of the Lord in a mirror, are being changed into the same image from glory to glory, as from the Lord Spirit.

The Holy Spirit lives in our spirit. When we were born again, we gained a new identity and that identity resides in our spirit. There is one problem, however—hardness of heart. The heart is the connection between the spirit and the soul and because we have hardness of heart, it keeps us from seeing who we are in the spirit. In our spirit we are totally free, for it is there that the Spirit of the Lord lives, and where He lives, there is freedom.

Thus, we see that the problem isn't in our spirit, it is in our soul which is our mind, will, and emotions. In our mind, will, and emotions, we are still not living total freedom. We still think the way our old man (our pre-salvation, un-regenerated spirit-man) thought in many areas. Our minds haven't been renewed as much as we would like to think. We are still having old man ways of feeling in our emotions. Even our will isn't free and it shows in our desires and decisions.

Paul writes in this passage that when our heart turns to the Lord in these areas, the veil is taken away and we are able to see ourselves in the spirit. We can behold the glory of the Lord in a mirror. We can start seeing ourselves the way the Spirit sees us. He sees us as the glory of the Lord. We are the ones who have been set aside to show the works of God on this planet so that others can see Him through us.

If we can but see who we really are, then the Spirit can start changing us to become like that image and conform us to who we are in Christ Jesus. The reason we know that it is a process is that it says from "glory to glory." We are going from one area in our lives that shows the Lord's work through us to other areas in our lives that God can move through. It is a process of growth as the Holy Spirit convicts us and shows us how to grow.

Eventually, we will be so submitted and conformed that others no longer see us but Him. Isn't that the goal of the Christian life? What seems to be the hindrance to this process? This verse reveals the answer.

2 Corinthians 4:7

But we have this treasure in earthen vessels, so that the excellence of the power may be of God, and not from us

We have this treasure in "dirt pots." God is doing a great work in simple vessels. It is that excellence which is so thrilling in us, and such a beautiful thing God is doing. He is using us to house and carry the God of gods to people on earth; it is nothing we have done so we can brag on ourselves, but something powerful that He has done so we can brag on Him. We can be used by God to bring Him and all that He is to others. If only we will yield and submit to the process of getting rid of our fleshly hindrances. Then true fulfillment can happen.

John 14:25-26

I have spoken these things to you, abiding with you; but the Comforter, the Holy Spirit, whom the Father will send in My name, He shall teach you all things and shall remind you of all things that I said to you.

The Holy Spirit is the one who teaches us everything we need to know. He imparts revelation. He gives us everything pertaining to life and godliness (2 Peter 1:3). We can trust Him to show us what we need when we need it (or before). It is like having Jesus walking inside us instead of walking beside us. We will be reminded of what Jesus taught us by the Holy Spirit. He is seeing us as the vessel of all God has for mankind.

And not just that, but He will guide us into the truth we need to combat the lies we believe and the lies the world promotes.

John 16:13-15

But when that One comes, the Spirit of Truth, He will guide you into all Truth, for He will not speak from Himself, but whatever He hears, He will speak; and He will announce the coming things to you. That One will glorify Me, for He will receive from Mine and will announce to you. All things which the Father has are Mine. For this reason, I said that He receives from Mine, and will announce to you.

The Holy Spirit is the connection we have with Jesus Christ. Everything Jesus had has been given to us through the Holy Spirit. He brings us revelation and announces the things of God to us. The Holy Spirit is constantly with us and speaking to us. He is the One that guides us into all the truth of the Father. If only we will listen to Him.

The Holy Spirit gives us all the manifestations of God. 1 Corinthians 12 and 14 tell of how the manifestations of the Spirit are to function in our lives. The big thing to see is that He is still working in us today and wants very badly to be able to have us available for all the work that needs to be accomplished.

He sees us as vessels to carry the Father and all He is to people on the earth. He knows we are just vessels of clay that need to be molded and conformed. He never sees me as inadequate or insignificant. I may be inadequate in my flesh, but in the spirit (where the true me lives) I am totally empowered and valued.

I had no idea how to see the Holy Spirit and how to think of Him until I was baptized into the Holy Spirit. He wasn't a person to me before, but some mystical being that I couldn't comprehend, let alone have a relationship with. When I saw that there was an aspect of my life that wasn't able to be used of God, I knew I had to change. Actually asking the Holy Spirit to do something was a foreign concept to me. When I was baptized into Him, He no longer was just on the inside of me, but was on the outside and was able to touch other people through me. That changed my view of Him and how I saw Him in me and working through me. I now can be used of the Holy Spirit.

Most Christians I have met do not think God can use them. They have bought the lie that they are worthless or unusable. If only they would see who they are in the spirit and let the Holy Spirit guide them into the truth. God doesn't make junk!

Others

It gets tricky trying to see how others see us. Instead of trying to untie that tangled knot, let's start looking at how they should see us.

We know that how others see us affects the way we think and act. We are all very susceptible to the influence other people have in our lives. In our ministry of helping people get set free from life's damage and difficulties, we have found that most problems come to us as lies we received between the ages of one through seven. Most of that comes as we are trying to please people and make judgments against ourselves that we are unworthy or inadequate. What they tell us about how they see us affects us in great depths of our souls.

We become very focused on ourselves because of all that damage. We are still trying to get attention or healing from the pain in our lives. We are still trying to gain acceptance and cancel rejection. It is amazing how many twisted things we do just to gain a good view of ourselves.

There is one area of our lives that we should be looking at instead. We should, as Christians, be looking at the reverse of the situation. We should be looking at the influence we can have in other people's lives. What can we do to help them see themselves the right way? Can we actually affect others so that they can walk the path God has for them? Yes, we can. In fact, we must.

If Christians would start thinking of others instead of being highly self-centered, the results would be amazing. We could effectively influence so many people into experiencing the freedom of our Lord and their true identity. We have huge power that is basically untapped in our times. Here's hoping we understand and receive the concept.

Acts 1:8

> ...but you will receive power, the Holy Spirit coming upon you, and you will be witnesses of Me both in Jerusalem, and in all Judea, and Samaria, and to the end of the earth.

Receiving power to become a witness on the earth is a well-known teaching from this passage. We know we need the power of the Holy Spirit to witness to people. But that isn't what this says. Jesus says you will be a witness. It didn't say you were going to be a good witness.

Most people witness to others about their weaknesses and defeats. They tell of all their problems and pitfalls, but very seldom do they tell people about their victories. That is why we need to walk in the Spirit to be a witness.

As we talk to the people we know or meet, what comes out of our mouths is what is truly happening in our lives. We complain and moan about the things that are happening in our lives and we often don't sound any different than the unbelievers we are talking to. We are being a witness to the fact that the Lord doesn't have any power in our lives and that we can't be set free from any of the problems. Why would anyone want to come to the Lord if He doesn't appear to have any power to set us free?

The beauty of what the Lord has done in our lives is that we can tell others about the victory that we have experienced. When we walk into their lives without trying to get anything from them, but have joy in our lives and walk in victory, we are being the "good witness" that we need to be. If we are free by the power of the Holy Spirit, that freedom can be seen and examined. That is when people will begin asking us about what they see in our lives that they want in theirs.

We should have the upper hand in every situation because we are those who are trusting in Jehovah. I have learned to walk in the joy of my Lord as I approach people and situations. I am automatically in the position of strength and am not susceptible to the attacks of people who want to keep me off balance. So often it is the case that people ask me about what I do for a living and it usually turns into an opportunity to bring freedom to their lives. They discover that there is hope for the problems in their lives.

This "witness" is one who walks in the victory and is an overcomer with a testimony about how God has shown Himself strong. That is what I want people to see in me.

2 Corinthians 5:18-20

And all things are from God, the One having reconciled us to Himself through Jesus Christ, and having given to us the ministry of reconciliation, as, that God was in Christ reconciling the world to Himself, not charging their deviations to them, and having put the Word of reconciliation in us. Then on behalf of Christ, we are ambassadors, as God is exhorting through us, we beseech on behalf of Christ, be reconciled to God.

God has given to us the ministry of reconciliation. The Father gave Jesus Christ to purchase us back to Himself. The sin that had come between us and had broken the relationship had been dealt with. The Father had done all that was needed to reconcile the relationship. If anyone came to Christ, their sins and deviations were no longer held against them. But something else happened that is important. The Word of Reconciliation was placed within us. What is that? The message that man can be reconciled to God. The broken relationship can be re-established. We can come back to having a relationship with the Father God.

This gives us a greater purpose in life. We become the representatives of Jehovah. We are not of this world, but we are in this world. Our job here is to be ambassadors for the Kingdom of God.

What does an ambassador do? The ambassadors of the United States live in another country that isn't the United States and they represent all that the United States is and does. If something is done to the ambassador, it is considered to be an act on the United States. Whatever the ambassador does is done as if the United States themselves did it. It is a huge responsibility and carries great power. This is why governmental leaders carry a tremendous responsibility to ensure that the right person is in that position. There are countries in which it is imperative to have the exact right person in that position. The ambassador could even start the next war, depending on what he does or how he responds.

The people who meet the ambassador judge the entire country on how the ambassador acts and what he says. This is exactly what our life is like. We are the representatives of the Lord God. How people see us is how they see the Lord. What they think of us is how they will think of Him. If we represent problems and sickness, then victory and healing are never understood as part of what God offers.

Reconciliation to God means recovering the relationship He really wanted clear from the beginning. Others must be able to see that reconciliation in our lives and hear it from our mouths. What we say and do is exactly what they will perceive as coming from God Himself.

Are we ready for the responsibility that is given to us? No wonder our "witness" isn't as effective as we wish it to be. We are talking something that we aren't fully living. We aren't representing all that the Lord has to offer. It is really important that we keep walking in deeper and deeper victory in our lives. The more we are free, the more His message will be delivered.

In other words, we need to know more about the country we are from. What is the culture of Heaven? That should be the culture we are living here. When my family and I were missionaries in Russia, we were confronted with an accusation. It was an accusation that has confronted many missionaries and, sadly, most have responded incorrectly. People have accused us of coming to their country to change their culture. Most missionaries work hard to deny it. I didn't. It was totally true that I was there to change their culture. I wasn't there to change it to an American culture, but to a Heavenly culture. Lord knows we don't need more defiled Americans; we need more sanctified citizens of Heaven.

John 13:34-35

> *I give a new commandment to you, that you should love one another; according as I loved you, you should also love one another. By this all shall know that you are My disciples, if you have love among one another.*

What a command Jesus gave to His disciples: Love each other. Wow! What would churches be like if we were doing that? The next chapter will be all about how to love, but now we are going to study the command to do so.

The first thing we must see is that Jesus told them to do what He already had done. We must love in the same way Jesus did. He is love. It is who He is, therefore it is what He does. We need to understand this. You can't do something to become something. You must be something and then the actions will come. He was telling them that they needed to become who God created them to be. Then they can operate the way God wants them to. Love, therefore, was proof of the inward change, showing up in the outward expression. And the target was each other before it was everyone else. The ones watching were those of the outside. Others must see us as a people who love.

And it goes even deeper than that. Jesus was a Rabbi. He selected personally chosen individuals to learn to walk in His particular kind of Judaism. This was called the rabbi's yoke. Remember the phrase, "Take My yoke upon you and learn of Me?" Jesus was saying that as His disciple, you reflect your rabbi in everything you do. He was telling His disciples that they were representatives of His walk with the Father. In essence, He was saying, to be of mine you must be like me. What you do reflects who I am. You must love one another because I am love and love is the gauge by which we are measured. Others must see you as love. Your love represents His.

Matthew 5:16

So let your light shine before men, so that they may see your good works, and may glorify your Father in Heaven.

When we shine the light of the spirit realm into the realm of men so that they may see it, it is called the glory. When we shine the light that is in our spirits in such a way as to come through our souls, it will affect those around us.

Others must see the things of the spirit realm working out through our actions. Our actions come from how we see ourselves. We don't do things to become something, we act in accordance with how we see ourselves. When we are no longer thinking only of ourselves, our love will come out in expressions that become works. Those works are the things that others see. When they see our good works that show the effects of what the Spirit has done in us, they will acknowledge that the work is from God. God will be glorified.

The outcome of the natural expression of what is true inside of us will cause others to glorify God. Our works must be out of who we are and not out of religion that is trying to become something. We are holy, made that way by God. We act holy when we know who we are. If we try to act holy to become holy, it is a work of the flesh and the flesh has never been able to make anything holy. What a trap the church has been in for so long to try to act our way to God. Sorry, it just doesn't work that way.

When this passage says "your light" it tells us that each person has a unique expression of the Light of the Spirit. You have to shine in your own way, the way the Lord wants you to shine. We are not to be just locked in to how others shine or how they tell us to shine, but we need to obey the Spirit as He is guiding us into all truth.

Philippians 2:14-15

Do all things without murmurings and disputing, that you may be blameless and harmless, children of God, without fault in the midst of a crooked generation, even having been perverted, among whom you shine as luminaries in the world.

We have to be careful with how we respond to people and situations in the world. We can't do things the way the world does them. They respond with complaining and passing blame. It is a response out of the damage of their souls. They are totally self-seeking and introspective. We must not be that way.

We have to respond as if we were children of God, because we are. The only way for the world to see the difference of what God has given us in our souls is to respond to things differently than they would. That always gets their attention because it is different than the norm. What is that famous expression? "Keep smiling. It makes people wonder what you are up to."

People can't handle it when we act outside of the way they expect us to. And they expect us to walk in the same degree of defeat they are walking in.

When we submit ourselves to Jesus, we let the light of the Spirit shine through us into their world. We shine like luminaries in their lives. It is their only hope. It also drives them crazy.

Ephesians 5:1

*Then become imitators of God, as beloved children,
and walk in love, even as Christ also loved us and
gave Himself for us, an offering and a sacrifice to
God for an odor of a sweet smell.*

Since we are children of God, we must act like Him and not like the world. How should others see me? They must see me as a representative of the Lord God Almighty. They must see me as an ambassador of His kingdom. We are the ones they can come to in order to contact God Himself. We are the ones who shine in this world of darkness and have hope for everyone and every situation. We are bringing the power of God to bear on the aspects of this world that are consuming people. Wouldn't our lives be different if this were how we acted around other people? Maybe that is the goal.

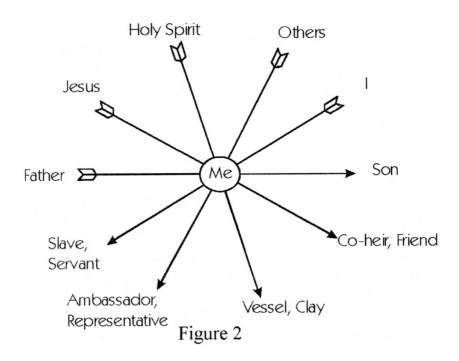

Figure 2

How Should I See Myself?

Now that we have seen how everyone else sees us, we need to look at the last person left. We need to see what the scripture says about how we should view ourselves.

This is a real problem considering how strongly we truly focus on ourselves. Self is the problem. "It's all about me." "When do I get mine?" "I have to take care of number One.' "If I don't take care of my interests, no one else will." "I can't trust anyone but myself." Do any of these expressions sound familiar?

We have all been wounded. Every last one of us is damaged. We learned at an early age to take care of ourselves. We have trusted in ourselves for our protection. We've had to take care of our own provision. We have even had to provide our own identity. Most of the things we see on TV or in movies, or even read in books and magazines is about how to foster and nurture our dependence on ourselves, and our independence from others.

The big problem with that philosophy is that we can't do it. We are not able to do everything for ourselves. When we fall short, we just confirm what others have said about us. We are inadequate and unworthy. Then we try to make someone else take care of us or try to find our answers in them. Rejection at that point is deadly. This system doesn't work very well. There must be another way of thinking.

In all our searching for someone to take care of us, we have neglected to look to the only One who is able—Jesus Christ, our covenant friend. When we put our problems in His hands, we can then go on with living the way He wants us to.

How should we be seeing ourselves? See Figure 2 on page 34. Others have a way of looking at us, but that isn't how we are to see ourselves. Focusing on "self" turns into a pride that isn't healthy. We cannot compare ourselves in any way to someone else. We are totally unique and have a unique calling on our lives. There is, however, in scripture a very strong consistent thread of how to see ourselves.

Mark 10:42-45

But having called them near, Jesus said to them, You know that those seeming to rule the nations lord it over them, and their great ones exercise authority over them. But it shall not be so among you, but whoever desires to become great among you shall be your servant. And whoever of you desires to become first, he shall be slave of all. For even the Son of Man did not come to be served, but to serve, and to give His life as a ransom for many.

A slave. We must continually see ourselves as slaves. Not conquered, forced slavery but willing and chosen slavery. So many have a real problem with saying this, but it is the exact way the Lord told these disciples that they should be.

When it comes to relationships, it is imperative that we see ourselves this way or we will always be comparing ourselves to others. That is a recipe for disaster.

If every person you come into contact with is someone you are to serve, would it change how you see them and treat them? If you are truly a slave, then it doesn't matter how they treat you or respond to you. You have nothing to prove and position to achieve. You just serve them.

It is extremely common to want to rule over people. So natural. But Jesus told them that He wanted them to do things supernaturally, not naturally. He was teaching them principles that operate in the spiritual realm that He wanted them to apply to this realm. Walk in the way of the Spirit. It is a higher set of laws and principles.

It was so important that the disciples saw Jesus walking by these principles. He did not come to be served even though He is the only One deserving to be served. Instead, He came to serve. Who did He serve? He served the Father and because of the love of the Father, He did everything necessary for the benefit of those the Father loved. Who do we serve? The Father. When we gain access to His heart we will love those He loves. We will have the attitude of a servant and not that of a lord.

Consider the story of the prodigal son. He was arrogant and had the right to demand His inheritance. He was standing like a son and a ruler over the land. His attitude reeked. He got what he demanded and it wasn't satisfying. He soon spent everything on himself and had nothing. The natural course of life happened and he found himself in a horrible situation. Only then did he humble himself.

As a humble person, he came to the father and asked to be a servant. The father was so delighted that he called for the instruments of covenant (a robe, a ring, the fatted calf, etc.) and entered into covenant with his son. His son kept the attitude of service and gained more than what he could have had through inheritance.

Even the older brother who didn't stray away had a bad attitude that was also one of selfishness. He couldn't understand the blessings his brother received because he had a works mentality. So much for the benefits of religion.

He compared himself with his brother that he had judged severely and deemed himself better. When his brother received preferred treatment, he was totally offended and shut off relationship with both his brother and his father. This is exactly what happens when we judge and when we are offended. Both of these areas will be discussed later in consequent chapters. This parable gives us insight into many different areas that we think are just the way life is supposed to be. How much we need to learn.

James 4:5

> "Or do you think that vainly the Scripture says, The spirit which has dwelt in us yearns to envy? But He gives greater grace. Because of this it says, "God sets Himself against proud ones, but He gives grace to humble ones." Then be subject to God. Resist the Devil, and he will flee from you. Draw near to God, and He will draw near to you. Cleanse your hands, sinners! And purify your hearts, double minded

ones! Be distressed, and mourn, and weep. Let your laughter be turned to mourning, and your joy into shame. Be humbled before the Lord, and He will exalt you."

God's plan all along has been to bless the humble. He doesn't want to compete with other gods. When we worship ourselves, and what we want and think, then He opposes us. He wants to give us His grace, but can't bless idolatry. We must be humbled before Him in every way. The more we are humble, the more He can use us. The reverse is also true. The more self-centered we are the less He can use us.

It is when we are totally submitted to Him that the devil will flee from us. Only then are we resisting in the right attitude and under the proper authority. It makes us much more powerful in the area of warfare if we are completely under the hand of the one with the true authority.

It is also the attitude of submission that brings us closer to Him. When we are humble, we can draw near to Him and He will draw near to us in a relationship that we've never known was possible. When we think we know it all and use our relationship with God as we use a vending machine (Drop in a prayer and pull the knob, expecting a blessing), then our walk with Him is limited and nothing compared to what we could have.

It takes humbling to examine the things in our lives that need to be changed. When we truly examine ourselves, we can see how dirty our hearts and hands really are. That is when He commands us to actually do the cleaning. We must acknowledge what we have done and take the responsibility for it. Only then is repentance true and not a ploy. When we start getting real with Him, He can start being our reality.

Only after all that are we going to be exalted. Even then we aren't exalted in men's eyes, but exalted in position of where God can use us. If we are the one to exalt ourselves, we are the ones taking all the life away from what we do. How much better to humble ourselves and let Him take care of the rest.

Galatians 5:13-16

For, brothers, you were called to freedom. Only do not use the freedom for an opening to the flesh. But through love serve one another. For the whole Law is fulfilled in one word, in this: "You shall love your neighbor as yourself." But if you bite and devour one another, be careful that you are not consumed by one another. But I say, walk in the Spirit, and you will not fulfill the lust of the flesh.

It is so important that we use the freedom we have in the right way. The only way according to this passage is to serve one another in love. It is appearing that being a servant is foremost on the Lord's mind. How are we to see ourselves? As servants and not as those who would bite and devour one another.

The Scripture is full of teaching on how to treat our fellow man. It doesn't include promoting ourselves over anyone. It does include serving each other and bringing each other into a greater relationship with our Lord. Why do we want to do this? Because it is the way the Master is pleased with us. We do it for Him, not out of duty, but out of pleasure for the heart of the One who is the most important.

Luke 17:7-10

But which of you having a slave plowing or feeding will say at once to him coming out of the field, Come, recline? But will he not say to him, Prepare something what I may eat, and having girded yourself, serve me until I eat and drink, and after these things you shall eat and drink? Does not he have thanks to that slave because he did the things commanded of him? I think not. So also when you have done all things commanded you, you say, We are unprofitable slaves, for we have done what we ought to do.

We have such a poor attitude so often. We are usually looking for someone to serve us and wait on us. As Americans, we are probably the worst in the world for this. We will serve in certain capacities as long as we have control over how we serve, where we serve, and whom we serve. When we are finished serving and have our religious quota taken care of, then we will sit down and let others wait on us and feel really good about ourselves.

When do we get ours? It will be our turn after we die. Do we deserve thanks? No. We were only doing what we were told to do. We still have too much emphasis on ourselves and our comfort.

In Romans 6:16-23, we are told that we are slaves to whom we obey. If we obey sin, we are slaves to sin. If we obey righteousness, we are slaves to righteousness. We are slaves no matter what. We just don't see it as such when we are worshipping ourselves. We think we value freedom at all costs. The only freedom we really value is freedom from restriction. We don't want anyone telling us what to do. Our independent attitude is somehow valued to the point that no one is able to tell anyone else what is right or wrong. That is a very slippery slope to stand on.

There has to be a path that God has called us to. When we walk that path, we are fulfilled. When we don't, we are continually searching to fill the void in us. The hollowness of self-worship has sucked the joy and purpose out of our lives. Then we wonder why we fight each other.

1 Thessalonians 1:9

For they themselves announce concerning us what kind of entrance we have to you, and how you had turned to God from the idols, to serve the true and living God

The only reason we have turned from idols (including ourselves) is to serve the true and living God. Our purpose in life is to be a servant to the Most High God. Everything else will prove itself to be futile and vain.

1 Peter 2:15-16

...because so is the will of God, doing good to silence the ignorance of foolish men; as free, and not having freedom as a cover of evil, but as slaves of God.

Our Freedom is in our slavery. The more we see ourselves as truly being slaves to God, the more freedom we will experience.

How are we to see ourselves as far as relationships are concerned? As slaves of God and servants to those He has created. If we can keep this view in mind, all other areas of relationship will fall into place. Rule number 1: I am a slave. Rule number 2: if all else fails, see Rule number 1. See Figure 2, page 34.

CHAPTER TWO

HOW TO TRULY LOVE

Perhaps you've heard something like this before, "You get out there and love those people. That is how you prove you are a Christian. You have to love everyone unconditionally. If you don't you aren't a very good Christian!"

I have heard that so much that it made me a wreck. The entire time as I was growing up I heard these messages from the pulpit that told us to go love people and I would go try. Oh, how I would try. The first thing I would do is run into someone that was very diffi-cult to love. I would try to love them and be defeated soundly. The next week I would come back to church whimpering like a whipped puppy. The self-condemnation was complete. I was a complete fail-ure as a true Christian. I couldn't love.

As I have grown in the Lord, I have found that I was not alone in that endeavor. I have found very few people that were loving and knew how to love everyone they came in contact with. It drove me to find out how to love. If I couldn't figure out how to love people, then the Word wasn't working for me. There had to be an answer.

As a pastor, I found myself trying to teach people to go out and love, but still didn't have the answer as to how. I found myself in the same predicament as those pastors I had growing up. I found the need to do it and the scripture injunctions to do it and the drive to get others to do it to fulfill their Christian walk. I didn't want to do what was done to me, so I started a search that just about killed me before the revelation came. When it did come, there couldn't have been a better time.

I had been working on my ministry with men who struggle with lust and pornography. I had found the key to getting men set free from lust. I found that whom you lust you cannot love, and whom you love you cannot lust. Lust is taking from that person what I want for my gratification. Love is the opposite. Love is giving to that person what it is they need for their benefit. I can't give to them what they need and take from them what I want at the same time. Love was the key to breaking lust. Now I had a real dilemma. How can I get men set free from lust if I can't show them how to love? My crying out to Jesus increased in severity and frequency. I couldn't get it out of my mind.

Greater Love

There is a verse that is quoted quite often. I bet you could quote it if you have been in the church for any length of time or have at least seen Mel Gibson's movie The Passion of the Christ. It is John 15:13 and it starts like this: Greater love has no man than this. Can you complete it? The chances are, you continued with the words: than a man lay down his life for his friends. That is the way it is translated in every Bible I have ever found.

However, that isn't what is conveyed in the original Greek. When I saw it in Greek, it blew my mind. I was stunned. We had missed the complete understanding because we trusted the translation. Deeper study was needed for deeper revelation.

The word for life in that passage is the Greek word *psuche* which means soul. What a huge difference! If the way I have greater love is to lay down my physical life then I will have only one friend and I will have him for a very short time. If I have to prove my love by dying for someone, then I have a problem having greater love for other people in my life.

The word there isn't life, though. It is soul. The literal translation of that verse should be: Greater love has no man than this, that a man lay down his soul for his friends. So, if I knew what it meant to lay down my soul, I could have greater love. Now I was getting somewhere.

My soul is made up of my mind (how I think), my emotions (how I feel), and my will (what I want or choose). Thus, "laying down my soul" means that I lay down what I think, feel, and want for someone else. Interesting.

Let's say I have a friend named John. If I want to love John, then I will lay down my soul for him. Right? So that means that what I think is laid aside for what John thinks. What I feel is laid aside for what John feels. What I want is laid aside for what John wants. Doesn't that make sense? *No!* Not really.

What if I am thinking godly thoughts and John is thinking lustful thoughts? Do I lay down my thoughts for the thoughts that John has? What if John is feeling hate and anger? Do I lay down feelings of peace and joy for that? What if John wants to hurt people or go do drugs? Will I lay down godly desires for those kinds of horrible desires? I don't think that is what God had in mind.

The key to this principle is the fact that you don't lay down your soul *to* your friend, but you lay down your soul *for* your friend. Then the question is begging to be asked, "Where do I lay down my soul and what does that look like?" Good question.

There must be something else that God had in mind. I started complaining to the Lord about why He didn't teach on this subject since it was so important. He said He did. So I said, "I know you probably taught the disciples, but why didn't you have it written down in the Word so we could all get it?" He said He did. We had just missed it. Really? Where?

John 10:1-18

Verses 1 to 10 set the scene and help us understand what the Lord is talking about.

> *Truly, truly, I say to you, the one not entering through the door into the sheepfold, but going up by another way, that one is a thief and a plunderer. But the*

one entering through the door is the shepherd of the sheep. The doorkeeper opens to him, and the sheep hear his voice, and he calls his own sheep by name, and leads them out. And when he puts forth his own sheep, he goes in front of them, and the sheep follow him because they know his voice. Jesus spoke this allegory to them, but they did not know what it was which He spoke to them. Then Jesus again said to them, Truly, truly, I say to you that I am the door of the sheep. All who came before Me are thieves and plunderers, but the sheep did not hear them. I am the door. If anyone enters through Me, he will be saved, and will go in, and will go out, and will find pasture. The thief does not come except that he may steal. and kill, and destroy. I came that they may have life and may have it abundantly.

Jesus is using the commonly understood reference of shepherds and sheep to teach here. He knew they understood the things that were plain common knowledge. By using simple everyday things, He could bring to them depth of teaching in ways they could understand.

He starts by showing the way of God in our lives. There is a good way and there is a bad way. If anyone gets in by any other way, they are a thief and a plunderer. He uses God the Father and Himself interchangeably here. At first the Father is the door and Jesus is the shepherd. The doorkeeper opens the fold to Him and the sheep are safe. When they go out, the shepherd calls them by name and He leads them out. Then He goes in front of the sheep and they follow Him because they know His voice.

That is really cool except for the fact that sheep don't follow the voice of the shepherd. If you have a western understanding of sheep in any way you will know that sheep need to be herded from behind and driven to the right place. This parable doesn't seem to make sense. That is why God made border collies. Again, misunderstanding and lack of revelation often result from our not studying the right things.

The main type of sheep in Israel when this was written was Karakul sheep. They are quite different than the sheep that we see in our western culture. These sheep are raised differently than the kind we are used to. You need to be there when they are born and speak or sing or whistle to them. They need your care instantly and you must build a relationship with them. From that day forward, they will respond to your voice. They will be totally dependent upon you. You have to care for them. If you try to herd Karakul sheep, they will be terrified and possibly even die of a heart attack. You must lead them, not force them anywhere. Because they know the voice of the shepherd personally, they trust the shepherd and will not follow anyone else. They won't follow the voice of a thief. They will only follow the one they have relationship with. How cool.

The analogies here are amazing. When we are born again and totally dependent on Jesus, He speaks to us and builds a relationship with us. As we depend on Him, we are able to hear His voice and follow Him. If we are forced to follow another path, it will completely freak us out (which is what happens in many churches as they force people to follow legalism, heresies, men or other false teachings) and will incapacitate us, possibly even to death, as it robs us of the life He intended.

When I am talking to people who just can't hear His voice and don't know how to follow Him, I know that there is something wrong somewhere else. It isn't that Jesus isn't talking. Perhaps they have been damaged by Christians or have a judgment against God. Maybe they are even just plain disobedient and the Lord isn't telling them anything more until they do what he told them to do the last time He spoke to them. Whatever it is, I know that the Shepherd is speaking and leading, so there must be a problem in their hearing or obeying. Whatever it is, there is healing and hope for them to come to the point where they can hear and obey the voice of the Shepherd.

Jesus then shifts gears a little and tries to explain it in a much simpler way since they weren't getting it. He shows Himself as the door of the sheep. In those days when a shepherd had a sheepfold, he stood at the only opening and inspected each sheep as it came in for the night to see if it had cuts and bruises or burrs or things that needed to be tended to. Once the sheep were in the fold, the shepherd actually laid down in the opening and became the door of the fold. No one went in or out without the shepherd knowing about it. He knew that anyone who tried to get in the fold would have to be a thief or a plunderer.

What is cool is that the sheep don't hear a stranger's voice or follow them. The sheep that are under the care of the shepherd will come in and go out and will be saved and find good pasture. What an awesome promise for us.

Jesus reveals the nature of the thief that he will only kill, steal, or destroy. One of the best ways to know whom we are listening to is by their fingerprints. Is something killing you, stealing from you, or destroying you? That is the evidence of being under the hand of the thief. How do I know when it is Jesus? It brings life and that life isn't just a little but life abundantly. That really works for me.

All this teaching was set up for what He is about to teach us. This is the foundation for what comes next.

Back to the Subject

Verse 11 of this passage tells us so very much. We find the same problem that was in John 15:13. The word for "life" here is also the Greek word *psuche*—the soul. He is saying the Good Shepherd lays down His soul for the sheep. Jesus is setting an example of what it means to lay down one's soul. A good shepherd will lay down his soul.

In the next few verses, Jesus shows us the difference between a true shepherd and a hireling. A hireling will flee when a wolf comes. He is more concerned about himself than he is for the sheep. The shepherd, however, is more concerned for the sheep than he is for himself. His reward isn't the money that comes to a hireling. The difference is life and death for the sheep. It really matters to me who is in authority over me. Are they shepherds or hirelings? Will they truly fight for my life or will they run away when things get tough?

This sounds like the difference between lust and love. The hireling is in it for what he can get out of it. When it starts to cost him anything, he is long gone. When one loves, the object of his love is more important than himself because it matters to him concerning the object of his love. How does he get that kind of love? From somewhere else and not within himself. Flesh cannot do any better than make one a hireling. It requires something out of this world to make love happen.

Relationship Is the Key

We learn from the verse 14 in this passage that Jesus is the Good Shepherd and that He knows those that are His and He is known by the ones that are His. He has a relationship with them. He knows the dangers they are in and the prospect of their future. They have value to Him and are of such worth that He is willing to pay the price for their safety.

Jesus then says something that is astounding. In verse 15, He states: He knows the Father in the same way the Father knows Him. He has relationship with the Father that is intimate and open. He compares His relationship with the Father to His laying down His soul for the sheep. Where does he lay down His soul? He lays it down at the foot of the Father and picked up what the Father thought, felt, and wanted. He laid down His soul and picked up the soul of the Father. He got supernatural for the sheep from the One who is Love. God is love. When we pick up His attitude for someone, it will always be love. That is who He is, not just what He does. Since Jesus was operating as a man filled with the Holy Spirit, He showed us that we must do the same thing.

He then explains that it wasn't just for the disciples that He was willing to do this, but for others. He was going to lay down His soul for other common people, the Pharisees, the rest of the Jewish nation and, yes, even the Gentiles. With that statement, He was telling us that we can love all those in the world and not just the ones we have a natural affection for in the first place. We can actually love those outside our little comfortable box of acceptance and lay down our souls for them. We must lay down our souls and pick up the soul of the Father for more people. This is something that we can do for anyone if we will but choose to do so. Jesus even gave others the same full status that the disciples had. One flock, one shepherd. I am sure they didn't understand all the issues around what was being said. This is mind blowing.

Think about anyone in the world. Think of people you find difficult to love, perhaps sinners such as prostitutes, drug dealers, rapists, murderers. Maybe you have a problem loving terrorists and extremists. Maybe it is people of a different race or color that bother you. How about people who smell badly or are poor or unattractive? Maybe you have a problem loving people who are rich. There isn't a person on the planet that you can't love if you will go to the Father and lay down your soul for them.

"How does it work?" you ask. If you will go to the Father and lay down what you think of them, actually admit it and take your fingers off of the right to think that way, and stay long enough to pick up what the Father thinks of them, what do you think will happen? He will actually give you His thoughts for them. If you will lay down what you feel for them and pick up what the Father feels for them, what would be the difference? Are you willing to pay the price of actually feeling the Father's emotions for someone? Jesus had to do this for you. What would happen if you laid down your will at the feet of the Father, everything you want for that person, good or evil, what you want to see done to that person? Would there be a difference in what He wants and what you want? What do you think Jesus was doing in Gethsemane? He was saying to the Father, "Not my will, but Yours be done. It doesn't matter what I want, Father, only what You want is important." Do you see the significance?

The hardest part of this process is actually getting a grip on what we think, feel, and want for someone else. Just thinking about humbling ourselves isn't enough. You can't lay something down that you haven't gotten a grip on. To lay a pen down on the table, you have to actually grip it, take control over it and know what you are doing with it. Laying down our souls is the same thing. You have to actually get a grip on what you are thinking of a person before you can lay it down. You have to get a grip on the emotions you have for them and your desires for them. Only when you have taken a full account of your soul can you lay it down. This takes some real soul searching on your behalf. It requires breaking denial and coming to terms with your actual soulish activity toward a certain person. That means acknowledging your hurts and the sins you have committed toward them. You must totally expose your soul to the Father and get serious with Him. This will entail some real repentance on your part.

Laying down our souls at the feet of the Father and taking up His soul is profound. It isn't easy. It costs me my selfishness and opens me to feel the hurt and heartache the Father is feeling. I will be vulnerable to feeling someone's pain. I will be opening myself to all their hurts, anxieties and fears. It will be a heavy price. But when I do, I am putting myself in a position to help that person so they are truly benefited. That is love. Everything else is lust.

I hope now you can see why Jesus said that others will know we are Christians by our love for one another. He also told us the greatest commandment is to lay down our soul concerning the Father and pick up His soul in relationship. We must do it totally loving Him with all our heart, soul, mind, and strength. Why? Only then will we have the relationship with Him sufficiently to be able to love others. Since He is love, this is the only way to love others.

One of the biggest problems I used to have in ministry was to try to explain to men how to love their wives since that is the foremost commandment for husbands. Now I know how. Every husband must spend the time in the presence of the Father laying down their souls for their wives and taking up the soul of the Father for their wives so that the husbands can accurately portray the role of Jesus in their homes. Most men are fighting for their identity and their manhood. The real thing a man must do is to go the Father and humble himself, lay down what he thinks, feels, and wants about his wife and pick up what the Father thinks, feels, and wants. Then his relationship with his wife won't be one of trying to get what he can from her (lust, and it isn't always sexual), but one of a servant-hood authority, serving her and the family to the best of his ability. Only then will he actually feel fulfilled in his relationship instead of feeling cheated.

Seeing How It Works Both Directions

What Jesus said next is one of the most outlandish things I have ever heard. Verse 17 says: For this reason, my Father loves Me, because I lay down my soul. What! The Father had to have a reason to love Jesus? That doesn't sound right. But that is what it says. When I got understanding on this one it really thrilled me.

Jesus didn't have revelation of the love of the Father for Him *until He actually laid down His soul.* When He picked up the soul of the Father, He also picked up how much the Father loved Him. Here is how it was explained to me.

One day I heard this statement in my spirit, "Water pipes get wet." I know it doesn't sound like much, but it thrilled me. Here's why. Let's say you have a garden which needs to be watered. You have a water tank, but it is several yards away. What do you do? You run some water pipes from the tank to the garden. You put a valve on the end of them and there you have access to water for your garden. When you turn on the valve, water flows from the tank to the garden and doesn't waste any in between. What is wet all the time? The inside of the water pipe. Just because we don't see the water on the outside, we forget that on the inside, the pipe is constantly wet.

What the Father was telling me was that whatever He can get through me, He can get to me. If I will become the channel of His love for others so that He can water their garden, then I will also receive His love in a way that affects me. The same things work for finances. If I can be the channel of finance to others, then the Father can get the finances to me to do it. However, no matter what it is He is trying to get through me and to me, if I don't turn on the valve, the flow cannot happen.

So many people I know haven't a clue about the depth of love the Father has for them. They are so stuck on thinking of themselves, that they cannot understand the love God has for them, and through them, for others. Jesus understood the love of the Father for Him because He was willing to lay down His soul for the sheep.

Jesus then shows us how much our choices weigh on the mind of the Father. Even He had to take things to the Father and let the

Father love through Him. Jesus says that He lays down His soul that He may take it again. The soul He takes up again is a soul that is in unity and agreement with the Father. But He says that no one can take His soul from Him. No one can force anyone to lay down their soul. It has to be a choice. I have to willingly lay it down. I can't make anyone love. I can only point the way. Jesus said that He laid His soul down from Himself. He chose to lay it down and take it up again. Each of us has authority to lay down our souls and we have authority to take it up again. The invitation to do it has been extended to you. What are you going to do with it?

The last part of verse 18 is very insightful. Jesus said that He received this commandment from His Father. Yes, it is our choice, but it is also a command from the Father that we do so. He is commanding us to lay down our souls and take up the soul of the Father. Only in this way can the Father get His love to people on this planet. We must obey, even though the cost is high. It will cost us what we think, feel, and want. It will cost us our selfishness. It will cost us what it cost Jesus. He was willing to pay the cost. Are we?

John 13:37-38

Did the disciples get it? When Jesus taught it, did they understand? Apparently, they understood enough to try to use what He said incorrectly.

In John 13:31 to 36, Jesus is leaving the Last Supper, the Passover meal just before He went to Gethsemane and then the cross. He is talking to the disciples and tells them that He is going away. He says, "Yet a little while I am with you. You will seek me and, as I said to the Jews, Where I go you are not able to come." Then He gave them a huge command (that I hope you have a better understanding of now). He commanded them to love one another. Peter didn't make it all the way to the conclusion. He got stuck on the first thing Jesus said. He said, "Lord where do you go?" Jesus responded graciously knowing where Peter's head was, "Where I go you are not able to follow Me now, but afterwards you shall follow Me."

Peter's response to that gives me cause to believe that he had understood the term but didn't get revelation of the truth in it. He tried to prove his love for the Lord and therefore his ability to go wherever the Lord was going. "Why am I not able to follow You now? I will lay down my soul for You!"

Jesus answers in a very unique way. He actually challenges Peter's statement. "Will you really lay down your soul for Me?" Are you truly going to die to yourself and live for me? Are you going to lay down what you think, feel, and want and take up what the Father thinks, feels, and wants?" I can just hear Jesus telling him, "Indeed you will, but you aren't ready to do so right now. Instead you are going to have to come to the end of yourself. You are going to have to see that what you think, feel and want are not right. So, to help you get there, you will have to go through the process of denying me three times and seeing that you aren't all that tough right now. You can't do it in your flesh. You will have to learn that."

I wonder what we will have to go through to be able to truly lay down our souls for the Father's soul. How much will we have to see of our inability to do it before we are truly willing to lay down our souls? That is an interesting speculation. The truth is that the Father is very interested in doing whatever He needs to for us to come to that point. We must learn to respond to the things that are happening in our lives so we can come to that point. Are you ready for the ride?

The Ultimate Calling

You know what John 3:16 says. *For God so loved the world that He gave His only begotten son, that everyone believing into Him should not perish, but have everlasting life.* That is absolutely awesome. The story doesn't end there. Look at what 1 John 3:16 says. Here is the rest of the story.

> *By this we have known the love of God, because that One laid down His soul for us; and on behalf of the brothers we ought to lay down our souls.*

53

We are to be held accountable to walk like Jesus walked. In 1 Peter 2:21 it says, "For you were called to this, for even Christ suffered on our behalf, leaving behind an example for us, that you should follow in His steps." That one laid down His soul for us and we ought to lay down our souls for the brothers. That is really simple. Not easy, but simple. Our doing what we are supposed to do is completing the gospel message. What started in John 3:16 is fulfilled in 1 John 3:16.

After seeing what Jesus taught in John 10, the response of Peter in John 13 and the incredible thing spoken by John in John 15 about greater love, we should be able to see that we have a godly commission to go through the process of laying down our souls as a command from the Father. I don't see it as optional, but required.

In **Revelation 12:11** it says this:

And they overcame him because of the blood of the Lamb, and because of the Word of their testimony. And they did not love their soul even unto death.

It seems that even our warfare with the enemy is affected by our laying down our souls. When I have laid down my soul, there is nothing the enemy can do to me. God has all of me and it only matters what God thinks, feels, and wants. That makes me dead to me and alive to Him. There is nothing that makes the enemy more useless and weak than that. This is what makes the weapons of my warfare divinely empowered. I win. I like that!

The proof that Jesus knew what He was doing and that it is very important is in Matthew 20:28 that says:

Even as the Son of Man did not come to be served, but to serve, and to give His soul a ransom for many.

He knew that He needed to lay down His soul and make it the price that would set many free. We have to make the same commitment. We can see many others helped if only we will be willing to lay down our soul and actually love them with the love of the Father. What a calling! What a concept!

If every relationship we have is to be a love relationship, anything less is a lust relationship. Every lust relationship will be damaging and unfruitful. Love will determine every reaction we have and our relationships will live or die because of our love and the laying down of our soul.

CHAPTER THREE

THE FREEING POWER
OF FORGIVENESS

There are few topics that invoke such emotion as the topic of forgiveness. It is a subject of great opposition. People don't want to forgive someone who has hurt them. Even if the desire to forgive is there, forgiving isn't easy because they feel that the perpetrator will get away with hurting them. The sense of injustice is a very strong emotion and we don't want people to get away with injustice. That tells us just how little we really understand the principles and power of forgiveness.

When we hear of someone who has forgiven someone for a massive wrong, we are amazed. "How can they do that?" It is such a huge thing for someone to do that it boggles the mind.

I have seen people who have been raped, sexually abused as children, made to do indescribable things and damaged beyond belief forgive their perpetrators. The issue isn't that the person who hurt them gets away with it. That isn't it at all. The issue is getting set free from that person and the damage they have done. Forgiveness is stopping the damage once and for all.

When someone realizes the principles of forgiveness in scripture, the real question should be, "How can they not do it?" It is the same as if we heard about someone keeping a knife buried in his thigh. It is ludicrous to not have it removed. But we know people (most of us are those people) who walk around as if they had a knife sticking out of their leg and were being wounded over and over and never did anything about it.

That is why it is something that the Lord has continually taught on. We are going to examine this scripture and find the principles and the instructions to do something about it. We will have some very practical steps and ways of doing this radical thing called forgiveness.

I know that I was taught to "just forgive them." It didn't work. There seems to be a lot at work here that I didn't understand. Then I found out that the people that were teaching me to just forgive people couldn't forgive either. We heard such excuses as "You can forgive, but not forget. You'll always have to deal with that" or "I'll forgive him, but that doesn't mean I'll ever trust him again."

If that is all we can hope for, then no wonder we haven't ever forgiven anyone and it remains a mystery to us why we are still in bondage. What the Lord has for us is so much greater than what we have ever known in the flesh. Our flesh can't forgive. Forgiveness is a function of our spirit. That is why it is beyond anyone who would try to do it in their own strength. It requires God's hand.

I remember a woman we will call Mary. At the age of five, her father started molesting her nearly every night. As she got older, it turned into rape. When her brothers got older, he taught them and they would rape her as often as they pleased. It was her place in life to let them all do whatever they wanted. You can imagine how scarred and damaged she was. She let them because it kept them from using her little sister. She finally stopped them at the age of fifteen.

When I met her she had physical and soulish problems in abundance. She couldn't get healing until we walked her through forgiving her father and brothers (and husbands who continued the abuse). When she forgave them, it wasn't them who received the freedom, it was her. Mary no longer was continually being raped in her mind or life. She was finally free from them. The Lord came to her and she received healing from the pain in her past and then her body started receiving the healing God had for her. It was remarkable.

That said, there is no excuse to not forgive. It is a command for us, not a suggestion. Every command is for us to walk in the spirit. It is the same here. In fact, the command is very straight forward and unmistakable. Let's look at one.

Matthew 6:14-15

For if you forgive men their deviations, your heavenly Father will also forgive you. But if you will not forgive men their deviations, neither will your Father forgive your deviations.

This is the only thing that the Lord expands on after giving the disciples the Lord's Prayer. Of all the things covered in the Lord's Prayer, the only part He discusses is about forgiveness. All that was said during the prayer is "Forgive us our debts as we also forgive our debtors." Huh? There seems to be a dependency of receiving forgiveness based on our giving forgiveness.

Jesus knew He had to say more on the subject because of the depth of what was said. He went on then to make it even stronger. There is no doubt now as to what He meant in the prayer. The principle involved here is very important. Don't expect what you are not willing to give.

We believe that we should be forgiven, but we aren't willing to forgive others. They want the same thing we want, to be forgiven. Even if we don't think we deserve it, we still want it. The freedom that comes from being forgiven is astronomical. We want to feel that freedom. When it comes to those who have hurt us, we don't want them to have freedom. We want them to be locked into bondage. They don't deserve to be forgiven according to our accounting of justice.

It is interesting that we condemn others because of their actions, but we want people to understand our intensions. We didn't mean to hurt them. If they only understood what we were trying to do or what was happening in our lives at the time. But the people that hurt us are to be judged because of their actions and it doesn't really matter what was going on in their lives or what they intended. Our unforgiveness is born out of a strong sense of injustice against the laws that we live by, not necessarily the laws of the land, but the laws that we have established in our minds that govern how we treat people and how they are to treat us. If you don't think that is true, just look at every child having interaction with another child. How many times have we heard the sentence, "That's not fair?" It is amazing what rules have been established without any rules being established.

We set in motion in the spirit realm the exact things that happen to us, whether good or bad. It is our faith (or the lack of faith that becomes fear) that makes things happen in our lives. When we set unforgiveness in motion in the spirit realm, that is exactly what we receive. If we set in motion forgiveness, then forgiveness is applied to us. God has mercy on those that show mercy (Matthew 5:7) and doesn't have mercy for those that don't (James 2:13). What we promote into the spirit realm is what we are going to receive. Sowing and reaping is still one of the strongest laws in all of scripture.

It is the same with forgiveness. God wants us to forgive the wrongs that are done to us so they have no hold on us. It is the physics of the spirit realm applied to our lives in the natural so that the hurts and injustices don't have a hold on us. Bad things happen. It is up to us to respond in a way that keeps it from continually affecting us.

As strong as this seems, it still isn't even the greatest depth of God's language concerning this subject. This passage alone should be enough to convince us, but there is more to look at.

Matthew 18:21-22

Then coming up to Him, Peter said, Lord, how often shall my brother sin against me, and I forgive him? Until seven times? Jesus said to him, I do not say to you, Until seven times, but, Until seventy times seven.

This is the beginning of a deeper understanding. Notice the religious response Peter is giving the Lord. He thought he was really doing a big service for his brother for forgiving seven times. Wow, what a highly spiritual guy! Isn't that like most of us? We do a spiritual deed and really expect a pat on the back. We are hoping others see the great things we have done and suffered for God. Jesus didn't play along with him.

Seven times? Try seventy times seven! Jesus wasn't really trying to get them to count how many times they had forgiven. Looking deeper into this passage and the principles involved, we can see what He was really saying.

Forgiving 490 times isn't just per person, but per specific act. Imagine someone slapping you on the cheek. You look them straight in the eye and say, "I forgive you. That's one!" They then proceed to slap you again. "That's two." On and on they go, 26, 43, 92, 157, 275, 316, 409, 487, 488, 489! Then just as you got to 489 they stop slapping you and then they kick you in the shin. "That's one!" Do you think keeping a running tally is going to help you at this point?

Even if it was per person, the Bible tells us to not let the sun go down on your wrath. So the list is at least per person per day.

What if it is a combination—per person, per offence, per day. We would be worn out just trying to keep track of all the sins done against us. It seems easier to just forgive.

The Lord was trying to make a point. Religion tries to keep score. The more we forgive, the more spiritual we think we are and it is all about how we look. If it isn't about religion, however, but about people and loving them, then forgiveness is very important. It is about others and how to bring the things of God to them. It is about how we are channels of God's love, life, and power to the world around us.

After such a stark beginning, Jesus then goes on to tell the rest of the story.

Matthew 18:23-24

Because of this the kingdom of Heaven has been compared to a man, a king, who desired to take account with his slaves. And he having begun to reckon, one debtor of ten thousand talents was brought near to him.

What an interesting beginning! How many men would have to take account of the slaves in his household and what they owed him? He must have a huge kingdom! But one was brought to him that owed him 10,000 talents! It is astronomical that *anyone* would be able to rack up that much debt, let alone a slave. Let's look at the sum.

A talent was 3000 temple shekels coming to around 75 pounds of gold. That works out to 900 troy ounces. The day of this writing, gold was worth $813.50 per oz. That makes every talent worth $732,150.00. Take that times 10,000 talents and you have $7,321,500,000.00. That is 7.3 billion dollars. And that is troy ounces. Back in biblical days, there weren't troy ounces and that would make 1200 ounces. Work that out and you will get $9,762,000,000.00 or 9.7 billion dollars. That seems to me to be a very large amount.

So here a king who finds a slave that he owns owing him over 9 billion dollars. What would you do?

The mystery would be how a slave got into debt for such an amount! Even if he was steward of his house, he couldn't rack up that kind of debt. The Lord was trying to get his audience to see a debt that was unobtainable.

The term "ten thousand" is an idiom meaning to be beyond ability to count or fathom. In the book *Ben Hur* by Lew Wallace, the vast amount Ben Hur discovered he owned (and that made him the richest man in the known world) was a staggering 673 talents—a little short of 10,000!

Matthew 18:25

But he not having any to repay, the lord commanded him to be sold, also his wife and children, and all things, as much as he had, even to pay back.

This is almost as amazing as the debt. What could possibly be gained by this. This slave wasn't worth anything compared to the debt. The fact, however, was that it would cost him absolutely everything towards the debt. He couldn't pay it back if he tried for the rest of his life. But that isn't the best part!

Matthew 18:26

Then having fallen down, the slave bowed the knee to him, saying, Lord, have patience with me, and I will pay all to you.

What?! This is astonishing arrogance! How was he going to pay? What kind of patience would it take to let him? But it even gets better!

Matthew 18:27

And being filled with pity, the lord of that slave released him and forgave him the debt.

He did it! The king actually forgave the debt! Isn't that an interesting way to put it? To forgive the debt? Can you imagine the awe in everyone around to have such a huge amount forgiven this man?

How would you respond? This man has amazing courage to even ask that he be given time to pay, but he had no idea the debt would be forgiven.

I can just see this king and his way of thinking. "If I destroy him and his family, I can make up a little of the debt, but if I forgive him, I will gain a very loyal subject for the rest of his life. I will have this kind of mercy in my legacy forever. Everyone will be able to see how much grace I have shown."

That would be logical. Do an extraordinary act and have it laid to your account. However, don't forget that he is still the slave of the king. The only thing that has changed is the debt is gone. That is no small thing, but his identity is the same.

Did that phenomenal act of mercy change the man? Let's look.

Matthew 18:28-29

But having gone out, that slave found one of his fellow slaves who owed him a hundred denarii. And seizing him, he choked him, saying, Pay me whatever you owe. Then having fallen down at his feet, his fellow slave begged him, saying, Have patience with me, and I will pay all to you.

Another debt. This one is for 100 denarii. A denarius was about one day's wage. Remember the parable of the workers being sent out into the field. Everyone was very glad to get a denarius for a day's work (Matthew 20:2). Let's use that for a way of figuring.

Let's say, for ease of math, a normal day's wage is $100 (that would be about $12.50 an hour). Take that times 100 days' wages is $10,000.00. That is a lot of money, but it is obtainable to pay that debt back. This gives us insight into the personality of many of us reading this right now since we owe that, if not more in many ways (don't make me bring up mortgages and car payments).

I have been in debt for that and more a few times in my life and each time I was able to pay it back and get caught up.

To owe this amount is serious. It was a serious deal between these two men, but it wasn't insurmountable. This first slave had just been forgiven a 9.7-billion-dollar debt. How do you think you would respond to this situation now? How did he? He choked him! He demanded payment immediately!

The second slave responded the same way the first slave did. He humbled himself and asked for time. The difference was, the second slave was actually able to pay the first one and the first one wasn't able to pay at all.

But then it gets worse!

Matthew 18:30

But he would not, but having gone away he threw him into prison until he should pay back the amount owing.

Debtors prison wasn't a laughing matter. You were thrown into prison and were used as slave labor. The prison got half of your money and you were kept alive to be able to work. The other half went towards the debt. Nothing went to your family. None of that mattered; it was strictly business. You had to work off your debt no matter what it took or no matter how long. This was a heartless, unfeeling way of dealing with the debt.

This gives us insight into being to be shrewd and calculating. He took a little grace and translated it into invulnerability. He looked as if he thought he was untouchable. What a tragedy. None of the kindness shown to him had affected him into positive change. The scum he was that caused his huge debt is still the scum that is damaging those around him.

Not to fear, people don't get away with what they think they do.

Matthew 18:31

But his fellow slaves, seeing the things happening, they were greatly grieved. And having come they reported to their lord all the things happening.

Busted! The one who had the authority to do whatever he wants to has just found out. What he had intended as a deed that helped people think kindly of him has been twisted into the king being an accomplice to this act of cruelty. Trouble was coming home.

Matthew 18:32-34

Then having called him near, his lord said to him, Wicked slave! I forgave you all that debt, since you begged me. Ought you not also to have mercy on your fellow slave, as I also had mercy? And being angry, his lord delivered him up to the tormentors until he pay back all that debt to him.

It is overwhelming what the king does. He calls in the first slave and holds him accountable for how he acted to the second slave. He tells him how he should have learned from the first experience. He should have learned the power of mercy and forgiveness. He should have known it because he experienced it firsthand. But he didn't and now the whole experience has been soiled.

All the goodness and kindness that was shown has been negated. What was a beautiful tale worth telling people is now a dark tale of grief and woe.

The king did something here that is very heavy. Because of the lack of forgiveness on the part of the first slave, the original debt has been re-established! The sentence that had been pronounced first has been altered. Before there wasn't any personal torture involved, but now there is. This isn't just debtors prison, this is the tormentors. Everything has turned bleak and foreboding.

If this was only a story, we could chalk it up to just being a dark story with some kind of moral to it. There is so much more to it. There are implications here that are staggering to say the least.

Matthew 18:35

So also My heavenly Father will do to you unless each of you from your hearts forgive his brother their deviations.

Suddenly Jesus turns this from a story into a practical application that shoots each of us straight to the heart.

The king is the Heavenly Father. We are the first slave. Our debt is insurmountable. We have sin before the Holy God of the Universe and there is absolutely no way to pay the debt. Out of His goodness, mercy, and kindness, in an act that shows the greatness of His grace and love toward us, He has forgiven our debt.

Doesn't it look familiar? When confronted with our sin we try to bargain our way out of it. "I will repay," we try to negotiate. Really? How? With what? Everything you are and have is tainted and worthless. As we plead with Him, He just forgives the debt. Unreal!

Do we know how much debt we have been forgiven? I doubt it. If only we could get a glimpse of the depth of our sin and the price that was needed to pay for it. We have become cocky and over confident before Him. How does it show? In our relationship with others.

If we don't forgive the debt others owe us, we are in trouble. Sure, others have really hurt us. There is an actual debt that they have accrued. What should we do about it? There is nothing here about getting paid or even making sure the others do the paying. The only thing here is the need for me to forgive their debt. It isn't that they need my forgiveness, even though that is true; it is about the need I have to forgive it. I have the need to show the King that I have learned how to do what He did.

When I see people who don't want to forgive, I know I have someone in front of me who doesn't know the extent of his debt that has been forgiven. *When we don't forgive, we are saying that the debt others have toward us is greater than the debt we had once before God.*

When we think this way, then we are believing the hurts others have caused us are greater than the pain our sin caused the Father in giving His Son, and the pain Jesus went through on the cross for us. What an elevated view we have of ourselves. We believed our pain is the greatest in the universe and must be dealt with in a manner that is both grandiose and emotionally satisfying. The problem with this is that it is never satisfying.

The greatest implication is the hardest one to wrap our brains around. It literally says that if we don't forgive, then the Heavenly Father will re-establish our former debt back on us. Our faith is for unforgiveness and that is what we will get. Is unforgiveness worth the cost of our salvation? How deeply are we prepared to pay for others to pay for their sins against us?

It is amazing how strong our view of ourselves is and how much we hold ourselves over everyone else in the world. In actuality we should be in great fear of not forgiving. The consequences are higher than we should be willing to pay.

The Mechanics Behind Forgiveness

As we examine how forgiveness (and the lack of it) works, we will be able to see what happens in the spirit realm. When we see how it really works, we will be able to understand why we need to forgive so badly.

Let's build a scenario to help us understand where we are going and the principles involved.

Fred and Tom will be our players. Fred did something wrong to Tom and hurt him pretty badly. There was lots of damage done and Fred was the instigator. For the sake of our story, let's just say that Fred is totally the one who is doing the wrong. Tom has done nothing wrong and is merely the recipient of the wrongs done.

We can use all the normal language to describe these guys. Fred is evil and Tom is righteous, Fred is bad and Tom is good, however you wish to talk about them. As soon as we use these terms, though, we tend to relate only to Tom, and Fred then becomes someone who has hurt us.

It is easy to see that the sin rests on Fred. He did what was wrong. The sin is on him. We come to that picture very easily. The actual truth is that through the interaction, Fred and Tom are linked. There are ties between them. Tom has some very tough choices to make.

Because of the trauma done to him, Tom now has a tendency to focus on Fred and wants to see justice done. Tom's life is now consumed with his pain and the need to see Fred pay for the things he has done. On the other hand, Fred can walk away without even worrying about what he did. He can forget that he ever did anything against Tom.

Tom can't seem to forget about it. As long as the sin is current in Tom's mind, it is as if Fred hurt him again every day. This is why so many of the traumas we have lived seem as if they were done to us yesterday. As long as we are rehearsing them or haven't dealt with them completely, they are still real and fresh.

Then comes the command to forgive. That makes things very interesting. If Tom doesn't forgive, then he is in sin. There are no differences between sins, sin is sin (except sexual sin according to 1 Corinthians 6:18, but that is a different story for a different time). Tom's unforgiveness is just as much sin as Fred's misconduct. Now the sin is on both of them and they are linked. There is a bond between them. These bonds are called soul ties. Neither one is free; both are bound up to these interactions.

If Fred repents before God, he will be forgiven. His sin can be removed. For repentance to be complete, Fred would need to go to Tom and ask him for forgiveness. Now Tom is in real trouble. If He chooses to not forgive Fred, then the only one with the sin on him in this situation is Tom!

Our Creator knew these principles would be in effect and how they would play out in our lives. To take care of us completely, He gave us the ability to forgive.

To do things correctly, Tom should have forgiven Fred almost immediately. Tom would have been released from the trauma of continual emotional damage. To forgive according to scripture, one must completely turn the perpetrator over to God. That would mean that the one who had been sinned against would have to lay down what he thought of the perpetrator, what he felt about the perpetrator, and what he desired about the perpetrator. He would have to lay down his soul at the feet of the Father and take up the soul of the Father for him like we talked about in the last chapter. That is why Jesus tells us to love our enemies (Matthew 5:44 "But I say to you, love your enemies; bless those cursing you; do well to those hating you; and pray for those abusing and persecuting you").

When we do this, the perpetrator has no hold on us. The trauma he did is covered by the grace of God to us, through us, and in us.

It gives true eternal implications to the actions we have here on the earth. We are given the privilege to operate here as God would and using the principles that can only be done in the spirit realm by those who are true children of the Lord God.

To back up this idea with the Greek language, the word for forgive is usually the word *aphiemi*. It is a compound word made up of two other words—*apo* and *hiemi*. Apo means simply "off or away," *hiemi* means "to send." Together they mean "to send away or to send off." When a person forgives, they actual send away the sin off that person.

If Tom forgave Fred, then the sin that would have been so damaging to Tom would have been sent away so that it couldn't touch him or affect him in any way. Fred still had the sin on him until he repents before God and then God sends the sin away so that it has no lasting effect on him. This forgiveness thing is an amazing tool to release people from the damage of sin.

If only we could get people to see the freedom in this. Almost on a daily basis I meet with people who have been hurt in ways that are beyond imagination and, in the natural, they seem to have a right to not forgive those that hurt them so badly. But the perpetrator is hurting them again and again. When I lead them through true forgiveness, the freedom is stunning. One of the ladies I work with keeps telling me that we need to put a doctor's scale in our office because people leave with so much weight off their shoulders that they must have lost at least fifty pounds!

Another word for forgive is *apoluo*. It is almost like the first word having "off" as the prefix. The second part of the word is from the Greek word *Juo* that means "to loose" It shows the power of forgiveness in that it loses the judgment off a person. It shows a definite release from that which held a person captive.

The third word translated "forgive" in the Greek is *charizomai*. It comes from the root word *charis*, which is the word for grace. Grace is to give to someone what they don't deserve in a good sense. God's grace is what brought to us all that Jesus has done.

Now it is our turn to grace others. We need to give them something they don't deserve (freedom from our judicial condemnation). We are to demonstrate to others, including our enemies, the kind of grace that God shows us.

This shows that we are to have the character of God manifesting through us into the lives of others on this planet. If we are never put in the position of receiving trauma, then we wouldn't be living the kind of life Jesus lived. We know that the godly will suffer persecution. We also know that we are to suffer in life. When it happens we feel like God has forsaken us and that we are abandoned. Never!

God is just putting us in a position to be like Him and bring grace to those around us. We are given the power to send sin off people. If we are never put in the position to use it, then what good is it to have it? Now that we can see how it works, let's look at some of the scripture and see the deeper ways of God.

Matthew 5:23-24

Then if you offer your gift on the altar, and remember there that your brother has something against you, leave your gift there before the altar, and go. First, be reconciled to your brother, and then coming, offer your gift.

A break in a relationship is so deep that the Lord here is telling us that we can't worship Him with the kind of freedom we need to have. As long as there is something between us and someone else, He is telling us that we must first go and find the brother that has something against us and be reconciled. Then we can come to the Lord and worship will be free.

What would our church services be like if we first required people to be reconciled before they could join in worship? If there was a way to manage it without becoming the "spiritual police" over people, the effect would be staggering. If everyone in the church were totally reconciled to everyone else and there was no animosity between people, the ability for people to focus on Jesus would go through the roof! The unity experienced would be something we have never experienced before. We would be able to worship without hindrance, without limit. I am longing for that time.

I have found this to be true personally. As long as I have a judgment against someone, my ability to worship is hindered. I have had occasion to stop trying to worship and go to a brother and get things straightened out with him. My worship after that has always been extravagant.

But all this is if the Lord reminds me that someone has something against me. What about the other direction? What if it is others sinning against me?

Mark 11:25-26

And when you stand praying, if you have anything against anyone, forgive it, so that your Father in Heaven may also forgive your deviations. But if you do not forgive, neither will your Father in Heaven forgive your deviations.

What if my prayers were hindered because of my unforgiveness? How can we come before the Father looking for His grace when we aren't willing to give that grace to someone else? Both prayer and worship are hindered by our unforgiveness or lack of humility to go and deal with what we have done to people.

This is one of the reasons I am writing this book. We Christians don't seem to have a grip on the depth of consequences in our relationships. It seems that we can treat others in any way we want with impunity. We are confident that we are receiving forgiveness, but are unaware of the true principles at stake. We don't seem to understand the depth of the consequences of unforgiveness. What we do to others have repercussions in our own lives.

John 20:22-23

And saying this, He breathed on them and said to them, Receive the Holy Spirit. Of whomever you may forgive the sins, they are forgiven to them. Of whomever you hold, they have been held.

This moment was the giving of the Holy Spirit. It wasn't the baptism in the Holy Spirit; that would come a little later. This is when the Holy Spirit came for the indwelling. This is salvation. The Disciples were actually saved or born again at this time. They were given new life and things would be different from now on.

It is what Jesus says to them at such an auspicious occasion that is interesting. They now have the power to forgive sins and to retain sins. This is of a depth that probably really blew their collective minds.

What was being told to them? They now had the Holy Spirit living within them. Now they will be held accountable for what they do in every way. They can now walk in the spirit (which they couldn't do before) and they have the power that comes with it. The only thing Jesus told them about here was the power they had to forgive or retain sins in the lives of others.

We have been discussing forgiveness and I believe we have covered that pretty well. It is this retaining business that is problematic. We can forgive sins, but we can retain sins? Of course! There is a technical term for it that we should know. It's called "unforgiveness!"

If I don't send the sins off and help people receive freedom, then I am withholding my power to help them, and in that way I have retained their sins. In my judgment, I have bound them to their sins and I can't see them any differently. *Every time I see them I think of them as guilty and their identity to me is the sin they have done against me.* As long as I haven't forgiven them, and used the power I have to forgive, then I have withheld freedom from them and condemned them to bondage.

Please, don't take this too far. If they repent at any time, they will be set free from their sin. It is only in my eyes that they are in bondage. By how I treat them, I am continually putting them in the position of reliving the sin. How I treat people is extremely important to what they receive from the Lord. We must not underestimate how much unbelievers watch Christians. Our witness shows others about God's power in our lives. When we live differently from the world, it points others toward God.

A person can come to the Lord at any given time and receive forgiveness through their relationship with Him. That being said, it is still true that how I respond to them will affect how they see the Lord and how they respond to Him. I wish to neither over-emphasize nor understate the power we have in people's lives. Suffice it to say that we should in every way be careful and walk in the spirit in our relationships with others.

To say that forgiving sins isn't powerful would be to cut out the power of God in many ways. We now have the ability to apply the power of the spirit realm to the realm of mankind because we are at the same time both natural men and those born of the Spirit of God with a Heavenly Father. We have both earthly authority, by just being born on earth, and Heavenly authority, by being born from above (John 3:3). Whenever we walk in the Spirit, we are applying the principles of the spirit realm to our earthly realm. That elevates everything into the spirit and we can then live by much higher laws. What a heavy and heavenly responsibility. Need proof of that? Look at this:

Matthew 9:1-8

And, behold! They were bringing a paralytic lying on a cot to Him. And seeing their faith, Jesus said to the paralyzed one, Be comforted, child. Your sins have been forgiven. And, behold, some of the scribes said within themselves, This One blasphemes. And seeing their thoughts, Jesus said, Why do you think evil in your hearts? For what is easier, to say, Your

> *sins are forgiven, or to say, Rise up and walk? But*
> *that you may know that the Son of Man has author-*
> *ity on earth to forgive sins, then He said to the par-*
> *alytic, Rising up, lift up your cot and go to your*
> *house. And rising up, he went away to his house.*
> *And seeing, the crowds marveled, and they glorified*
> *God, the One giving such authority to men.*

What a fascinating story! Jesus perceived something that we should pay attention to. This man's sickness was a direct by-product of sin in his life. Because of the words "be comforted" we can reasonably see that he had held himself guilty and responsible for something that had happened. He probably felt he deserved this sickness and didn't have much hope of ever getting out of it.

This story tells us so much in many ways. When dealing with sick people, we have a tendency to just see the sickness and not the cause or root of the sickness. But, if we learn to deal with the root, then we can get rid of the fruit.

The conversation became very interesting when the religious people in the room were horrified because He told the man his sins had been forgiven. In Mark 2 in the telling of this story, it is recorded that they said, "Why does this one speak blasphemies this way? Who is able to forgive sins, except One, God?" They weren't totally wrong. Only those who have the authority from the Spirit of God can. But we do. It was given when the Holy Spirit was given.

Jesus' challenge to them now is deep and personal. "Which is easier to say, 'your sins are forgiven' or 'rise up and walk'?" Neither one was possible to them. They had neither the authority to forgive sins or the power to heal him. Talk about standing there with egg on your face! Then it got worse for them.

"But that you may know that the Son of Man has authority on earth to forgive sins," then He said to the paralytic, "Rising up, lift up your cot and go to your house," He showed them that He had power and authority to do both. What a bold confrontation! "You can't, but I can. What are you going to do about it?" If only one of them asked Him for this power and authority, we would have seen salvation coming to someone in the hierarchy of Jerusalem. It is amazing to me how much we miss because of pride.

The crowds didn't miss the exchange. They glorified God because He had given such authority to men. They didn't say Jesus was God on earth, but that He was a man and that God had given this authority to Him.

Are we paying attention? When the Holy Spirit was given, so was the power and authority to do what Jesus did. That includes the power to forgive sins. We have a huge responsibility to the people in our lives to forgive them for the things they have done to us. *It actually goes a little further as we have the authority to stand as proxy and deliver the forgiveness of God to people.*

Jesus didn't walk around forgiving people indiscriminately (just the ones the Father brought to Him about this issue.) Are we listening to the Holy Spirit enough to be able to speak the power of God into someone's life to tell him he is forgiven? Makes one think, doesn't it?

The Victim

It is just as important to know how not to see ourselves as it is to see how we should see ourselves. We have been very quick to take on the identity of a "victim." We may have been the recipients of some bad act and we are looking for someone to have some sympathy. It seems important that others see us in our state of damage and despair. When they see how badly we've been treated, then our cause for justice is wholly justified and we look good and the attacker looks evil. Court has been set up and the perpetrator is proven to be wrong. All our judgments are justified and we get the sympathy vote, as it were.

The problem with this kind of scenario is: when do we stop being the victim? Never. Every time it seems that the perpetrator might be getting off the hook, we rehearse the crime and prove ourselves as victims all over again. That means we live it all over again and the trauma is renewed. We actually tell the stories for one-upmanship. "You think that was bad, you should have seen what happened to me!"

I have dealt with people who as little kids were victims of true abuse. One of my close friends in ministry deals regularly with victims of Satanic Ritual Abuse and Masonic Ritual Abuse. These are true victims of incredibly horrible tortures and mental programming. When I counsel people with this background, I steer them away from a victim mentality. If they keep it, they will never be able to be free from the trauma and it will seem as if they are being traumatized every day again.

The truth is not as we have seen it. Let's look at Tom and Fred again. Fred punched Tom in the face and called him all sorts of names. Who is the victim here? Fred is. Let me explain.

Tom is a believer in the Lord Jesus Christ. He has been given everything he needs in every way for everything pertaining to life and godliness. He can take his pain and the situation to the Lord personally and immediately (if he will). If he doesn't take it to the Lord, then he is taking it all on himself and he is hurting himself more than Fred ever could. It isn't what Fred has done that is important, but how Tom responds to the situation.

The victim is Fred because of who the real perpetrator is. Our common enemy, Satan, is behind the rage and damage that is happening in Fred. He has fanned the flames to the extent that Fred has acted against Tom who is a believer. That is extremely dangerous.

The God of the universe has put in motion laws that can never be ignored. One of those is "I will bless those that bless you and I will curse those who curse you (Genesis 12:3)." Who is in trouble? Fred! He has come against one who is blessed and that puts God himself against him. He is now cursed by God. That isn't good.

Fred has also let the enemy stir up his emotions against Tom and that in itself is deadly. The more emotions and judgments Fred has against Tom the less chances he has to come to the Lord. He will use Tom as a bad example of a Christian and that will have a tendency to keep him away from the Lord. A simple interaction between two people and eternal implications are now in play.

But it is how Tom sees things that is important. If he can truly see that Fred is being used of the enemy to attack him, then God's grace is given to him to handle the situation, (if he will just tap into it). If he responds correctly, he can humble himself before Fred and deal with the situation in a way that will probably take Fred by surprise. If he will immediately forgive him, and treat him as forgiven, Tom can introduce God into play here and the miracles that become available are amazing.

Tom can bring this all into the hands of the Spirit and things will be totally different. Tom's suffering will bring about an opportunity to take things out of the flesh and into the Spirit.

Tom can lay down his soul for Fred. Love your enemies is a command and a huge opportunity. He must lay down how he thinks of Fred, what he feels about Fred and what he wants concerning Fred. Seeing Fred through the eyes of the Lord is the key to the beginning of forgiving Fred. He must love him first. If he forgives Fred immediately there will be no damage to Tom's soul. He can be God's representative on the earth. He sees himself as the servant to be used to change Fred's life. Everything can be turned around and be used of God.

As long as Tom has a victim mentality, he can't be used of God as he should be. It is impossible to have a victim mentality and not be self-centered to a degree. If it is all about us, it can't be about others. God's whole plan of love is waylaid. No wonder relationships are so important to Him,

God's plan is for us to live this life in the Spirit and not in the flesh. To forgive requires walking in the spirit. The flesh cannot forgive. Let's go on to the practical steps of applying forgiveness.

How to Forgive

1. Deal with the pain

We must get Jesus involved in the process immediately. He is the only one who can do anything about this situation. We must take the pain to Him. It is really quite simple, but not always easy. We have lived with the pain for a long time and it has become a part of us, not a healthy part, but a part none the less. It is time to get honest and serious with our Lord.

Come to Him and tell Him, "I have been really hurt. I am in pain over this." Tell Him exactly how you feel. Tell Him about your anger and what the injustice did to you. Bring it all. Tell Him everything you have always wanted to tell someone. Let it all out. Examine your feelings and all that is within you. Bring it to Him and lay it at His feet. What we have is a relationship, not a religion. Your pain does matter to Him.

Remember the story about Mary? She had to come to the Lord and tell Him about how much she was in pain. She had to come to Him and trust Him for the inner healing. It was true that there was a vast injustice, but Mary couldn't continue living with the hurt. She had to turn it over to the Lord. He came to her and brought healing to her and freedom from the lies she received from the abuse. Forgiveness was only a part of the things she needed, but without it she couldn't have gone very far.

The one question you shouldn't ask is "Why?" "Why did this happen to me?" "Why didn't you stop it?" There is no way for the Lord to answer you. You couldn't handle the answer. Understand that you don't have enough understanding to deal with it. He is God. You aren't. There is no way you can have enough intelligence to understand all you would need to know to understand the answer. There is so much that you will have to just let Him carry it. He alone can handle it. You will have to trust Him for the rest.

Corrie Ten Boom was traveling with her father by train to Amsterdam one day. He was a watch repairman and carried large cases of watch parts to and from suppliers. As they were traveling she asked her father, "What is sex sin?" (She was only around eight years old at the time.) Her father thought for a few minutes and then asked her to pick up one of his watch cases. He even made her try. After a few minutes of futility, she told him that she couldn't carry them because they were too heavy for her. "The answer to your question is just like that case, Corrie. It is too heavy for you to carry right now. You are going to have to trust me to carry it for you until you get old enough to carry it yourself."

That is the question "Why?" in our lives. The Lord will have to grow us a lot for us to be able to handle the answer. The best thing is

78

to trust Him for the areas we can't understand and when we are able to handle it, He will open our understanding to the answer.

2. Lay down your soul

Go to the Lord about the people who have hurt you. Continue to lay down what you feel about them, what you desire for them and what you think about them. Stay before the Lord until you have taken up how He feels, desires, and thinks about that person. You must get to the point where you are loving them with the love of the Lord himself.

As the Lord shows you how He sees them, you will then be able to lay down how you've seen them in the past. With your pain in the Lord's hands, and your ability to see them the way the Lord does, you will be able to have insight into what is true in their lives. Your ability to love them takes away the sting of the injustice they have done to you.

3. Actually forgive them

This isn't just a forgive-them-by-faith thing, but an actual releasing them from the sin they have done against you. It will require the actual words spoken out of your mouth, "I forgive you." But even that isn't enough; you must state what you are forgiving them for. "Fred, I forgive you for stealing from me." It must include their name and the offence. Once you have given the pain to the Lord, and seen them the way the Lord sees them, then it is just a step in the process to send the sin off them.

It is in this step that the freedom is experienced. Take time here to let the Lord touch you in the process. You are doing a very spiritual thing and you need to see what is happening in the spirit realm. As you see them through the eyes of the Lord and release them from the sin that has come between you, you will then be able to do for them all the Lord would have you do.

There are yet more depths and levels to this understanding. We will be exploring them in the next chapter. There will be more practical things that are to be done and more understanding to achieve.

The principles here are full and solid. The next chapter will enhance your understanding of how things work in the spirit realm. This is so much more than just saying the words; there is a true spiritual release that happens.

4. Ask for exposure

Ask the Lord to reveal to you others that you need to forgive. Be prepared to be flooded with faces. The Lord is very powerful in these areas to show us the people we need to forgive. He knows how important it is and the effect it is having on us to not forgive.

When we ask Him, He is very faithful to show us each area of unforgiveness that is gumming up our soul and keeping us from the beauty of what He has intended for us. He will continually work with us to bring to our mind each one we need to forgive. Each one is helpful for getting our soul freed up to become who He called us to be, instead of who the pain has tried to make us. Until we are no longer influenced by the unforgiveness, we are owned by those who have hurt us. When we get rid of the chains that bind us, we are free to do all that the Lord would have us do. That is freedom.

5. Ask for forgiveness

It is one thing to forgive, but quite another to actually humble ourselves to ask for forgiveness. We know we have done things to hurt others. We keep hoping that they didn't notice or that they will just get over it. How seldom have I witnessed someone with the courage to go to someone else and ask to be forgiven?

Think of how much an impact it would be if people would take responsibility for their actions, whether intended or not. If people would not try to defend themselves and just own up to their actions, there would be so little left for people to be offended over. Nowhere in scripture does it justify us trying to defend ourselves. Instead we must humble ourselves and take ownership of what we have done. We must depend on the Lord to defend us or give us the grace to handle the consequences.

Self-justification is one of the greatest problems in the church today. Each one of us wants other people to realize how much they hurt us, but we are not willing to admit how much we hurt them. We justify our actions and dismiss what we have done as not important, even though the people we have hurt consider our actions to have life impacting importance. To us it wasn't a big deal, but to them it was huge. We then can say that they just blew it all out of proportion. What is wrong with those people? Then we turn around and do the exact same thing when others hurt us.

Let's say that Fred hurt Tom and was 95% wrong in the situation. Tom will feel quite justified to condemn Fred in every way. But Tom was responsible for the 5%. Tom needs to go to Fred and ask his forgiveness for what he did that was wrong. That doesn't justify what Fred did. On the contrary, it will actually help Fred receive responsibility for what he did because Tom was willing to take care of the part he was wrong in. If we will respond the way God tells us to, we will be able to bring the power of the Holy Spirit into situations that He couldn't have access to before. A little humbling on Tom's part could be the insertion that the Holy Spirit needs to bring Fred into conviction and possibly eternal salvation. All this because Tom was willing to humble himself and ask forgiveness even in the least of the offences.

6. Asking forgiveness from our Lord

When all these things are taken care of, then it is the easiest part to come to the Lord and ask for forgiveness. He is the only one who can totally forgive and it is His nature to do so. But He doesn't give it indiscriminately. He can only give it where we've allowed Him.

There is something that I have learned through ministering to people that is a huge benefit. When someone is working through issues with the Lord and we have him or her ask for forgiveness, we then ask the question, "What did He say?" It is amazing how many people ask the Lord for forgiveness and don't listen to the answer of the question. Isn't it rude to ask a question and not listen to the answer? People look shocked when we ask them that. "Just listen, did He forgive you?" When people stop to listen to the answer and they hear the Lord tell them that they are forgiven, then they never doubt again that they have been forgiven. It just makes sense.

CHAPTER FOUR

JUDGMENTS

Let's take forgiveness to an even deeper level. While scripture has a lot to teach us about forgiveness, specifically, the principles involved go much deeper when you consider judgments.

Judgments are when one person judges another with the intent of giving sentence or determining punishment or payment. When a wrong is done to a person, that person tends to view the perpetrator as guilty and therefore, must be sentenced to pay the price for that crime.

The guilty one doesn't necessarily feel the need to pay for it, but the one sinned against feels that need. Because of a strong sense of injustice, he believes he has the authority to pronounce that judgment on the perpetrator. He is concerned that the perpetrator is going to get away with it and that there should be some kind of payment.

This is so natural that people can't see anything wrong with it. It just seems right. Terrorists must be made to pay. Thieves, rapists, murderers, deceivers, all must pay for their actions in a perfect society and culture. Don't we all feel that way? Not at all. It really depends on the who and the what and how it hurt me personally. The ramifications are huge here and that is what we are going to look at.

Judgment automatically assumes many things. It doesn't need true authority; it makes up its own. It doesn't even need a written set of laws, just the hurts that are being felt by the actions of someone else. It assumes that our judgment has the ability to actually make the perpetrator hurt in the same way and level as he hurt us. It assumes that the perpetrator can pay and that it will take away the hurt. All these assumptions are wrong and have with them deceptions that are just as damaging as the original crime.

The Lord has given us in scripture the ways to keep judgment from destroying our lives. When we apply the principles, we can live in a way that is life-giving and not deadly. He didn't want us to be the one in judgment. He wants us to turn all that over to Him and let Him deal with it. What should we do with these situations? That is what makes us different from the world. We don't do things that seem natural, we do things that are supernatural. The freedom is amazing. Let's look into the Word and see how it works.

Matthew 7:1-2

Do not judge, that you may not be judged; for with whatever judgment you judge, you will be judged; and with whatever measure you measure, it will be measured again to you.

It is difficult to receive the simplest things put in front of us. This verse is a simple command. It isn't a suggestion. He outright commands us not to judge. It isn't something we are to think about or determine whether or not we should do. It is a command. And there are reasons He commanded us in this way—that you may not be judged.

His commands are always there to save our lives. He commands us to do things that will benefit us. It is His love that fuels His commands. He goes on to tell us that with the very judgments we judge, that is the judgment that we will be judged with. Without thinking about it, that sounds good. "I didn't do what that creep did." Sounds safe doesn't it?

Think about it and you will see that it isn't a good thing. When we judge, we are putting ourselves in the position of being under the scrutiny of deserving judgment. When we put ourselves in the position of judging, we say that we are righteous enough to compare our lives with the person that hurt us. If we have hurt anyone in any way, then we are in position to be judged and that is according to our own judgment. Whatever we have determined to be right to have happen to the one who hurt us, that is what we deserve to have happen to us. We are under the sentence we have handed out. Ouch.

It is confirmed in the next verses as God uses an illustration to teach us.

Matthew 7:3-5

But why do you look on the twig that is in the eye of your brother, but do not see the log in your eye? Or how will you say to your brother, Allow me to cast out the twig from your eye; and behold, the log is in your eye! Hypocrite, first cast the log out of your eye, and then you will see clearly to cast the twig out of the eye of your brother.

The principle of the log and twig has been a strong discussion for many years. It seems to be a favorite of people who are trying to get others to quit judging them, but then they forget about it when they desire to judge someone else.

When we are the victim, it is simple to see that the other person needs judgment. When we have done something against someone else, we don't like the scrutiny and tell people not to judge us. Seems so hypocritical, doesn't it? We don't like to be judged, but we seem to really like judging.

The Lord is strong in talking about how we can't seem to see straight to judge other people. It is all a matter of perspective.

For example, Fred has a log. Good-sized, solid, heavy. Quite a log. Tom has a twig. Not much to look at and not very impressive, it is just a twig. It is simple to see that Fred's chunk of wood is a lot bigger than Tom's. But the closer Tom's twig is to Tom's eye, the bigger it becomes in Tom's perspective. It doesn't take much to make Tom's twig bigger than Fred's log.

Now, put Tom's twig *in* Tom's eye. *Ouch!* The pain Tom is experiencing makes his twig huge! It is almost impossible to see around it. Pain makes perspective a whole different set of rules. Pain changes things. Suddenly Tom has the log and Fred's has been reduced to a simple twig. How can Tom expect to help Fred remove his twig when all he can see is the log that is causing him such great pain. A simple sliver is much more wood when it is stuck in our eye.

Once when I was working for my Dad as an electrician, I got a little reckless. I had to crawl in a tight place and use my hammer to punch a hole in a lath and plaster wall. Usually it wasn't a problem. But this time I was laying on my side in a false ceiling with only a flashlight for illumination. The whole place was choking with old dust and it was very uncomfortable.

As I swung the hammer, I could actually see the wood break and a piece of the lath board I hit broke off and was flung back at me. I saw the sliver go into my eye. It really hurt. I closed my eye and worked until I could leave using my good eye. I was useless after that. All I could think about was my eye and the pain I was experiencing.

We actually pulled the sliver out of my eye with a pair of tweezers. Even though the thing that caused my pain was gone, it still felt like it was in there. It took a long time for that to heal to the extent that I could work without pain. Every time I read Matthew 7, I emotionally experience it again. The twig in my eye consumes all my perspective. Pain will do that.

The illustration here is quite clear. How can we judge others when there is so much in our lives that is in danger of judgment? We need to be so humble that we aren't putting ourselves in the position of judging others. In that way we aren't putting ourselves in the position of being judged, we are just trusting in the Lord to pay for it all with the blood on the cross. Both the things that need to be judged in me and in others must be in the hands of our Lord.

If we don't judge others, then we aren't putting ourselves in the position of being judged. No wonder the Lord told us not to judge. What a freedom He is trying to get us to live in.

There are other scriptures that give us more detail and help us with this understanding. Look at this one.

Romans 2:1-2

Therefore, O man, you are without excuse, everyone who judges, for in that in which you judge the other, you condemn yourself, for you, those judging, practice the same things. But we know that the judgment of God is according to truth on those that practice such things.

When we judge someone, we determine the rules that we feel are to be lived by. The problem with that way of thinking is that we aren't able to live totally free from sin. When we sin we are doing the same thing that we have determined needs to be sentenced for condemnation. We actually agree with God in His view of condemning sin. However, He has done something about getting rid of sin and it has nothing to do with our purity of actions.

He gave the blood of Jesus Christ to pay for it. There isn't anyone that can stand before God based on his own actions. All it takes is one sin for us to be guilty of all sins. One break of God's law is enough to condemn the whole life. We rest on the truth that the blood of Jesus Christ cleanses us from all sin. We come before God knowing our sin is washed away. We thank Him for the grace given to us to set us free from the penalty of sin and death. How we thank and praise Him for His love toward us.

Then we judge someone. We change the rules that we live by. All of a sudden we have decided that it is by a person's actions that he or she should be judged. According to this passage, we have taken away all of our excuses. We condemn ourselves when we judge someone else. Since it is God who judges with the power of total purity, we stand before Him expecting Him to judge us according to how we have decided judgment should be done. We have changed the rules away from the way God wants to deal with sin. Look at the next verse.

Romans 2:3

And, O man, the one judging those practicing such things, and doing them, do you think that you will escape the judgment of God?

This verse shows us that when we determine the way judgment is supposed to work, God will extend His judgment toward us to comply. Do you really think you would be able to escape? What you really want is to have God's grace working toward you, but not toward anyone who would have hurt you. You don't want to extend God's grace toward someone who has done something against you. Since you are the most important thing in the universe, whoever hurt you must pay by a different scale than everyone else. They must pay for their actions.

But as far as you are concerned, you desire for grace to be set toward you and for God to forgive and understand your weaknesses. How do I know that? Look further into the passage.

Romans 2:4

Or do you despise the riches of His kindness, and the forbearance and the long-suffering, not knowing that the kindness of God leads you to repentance?

Do you look at the riches of God's kindness toward you and the long-suffering as being something given to you and not given to others? When you determine that grace isn't needed, you despise what God has done for you.

The Greek word for kindness is the word *chraystotays*. It would be best translated as usefulness. God is the only one that is useful for taking care of my sins. Nobody else could do anything about it. Only the blood of Jesus can wash away my sin. It is based completely on His grace and giving me a gift that I didn't deserve but was given because of love.

When we change the rules by which we operate, we negate the power of God to take care of our sin. We become the one who has to do something about our sin and we can't. We need to get back to the only way that things can work. He is the only one useful for dealing with my sin. I stand by grace. When others hurt me I must keep those rules working. I must give them the grace needed to set them free from my judgment and only then can God work in their lives and in mine.

Grace is when we give something to someone who doesn't deserve it. That is what happened to us. We don't deserve to be forgiven of our sins, but God's grace is so powerful that He wants to do something for us that is beyond what we would ever deserve. He brings us salvation because of His love, not because of what we deserve. Then He tells us to do the same for others. Let's look at it.

Ephesians 4:31-32

Let all bitterness, and anger, and wrath, and tumult, and evil speaking be put away from you, along with all evil things. And be kind to one another, tender-hearted, having forgiven one another, even as also God forgave you in Christ.

How does someone get rid of bitterness, anger, wrath, and all this bad stuff? It starts with us being kind to the other people and being tenderhearted. How do we get there? You have to go through the verse backward to get it. It starts with God forgiving us in Christ. As we are united with Christ we are given grace. The word for forgave here is the Greek word *charizomai*. It comes from the root word for grace. This word for forgiveness means to actually have grace for someone else. We must give them something good because of who we are, not because they deserve it. Grace can only come from God. When we let Him, He uses us to bring His grace to someone else. We then become the channels of who He is to someone else!

When we receive His forgiveness, we are then able to give it to others. That will give us the ability to be tender hearted toward them, no matter what they have done to us. The word for tender-hearted here is the Greek word *eusplachnos* and it means to have good, very deep compassion for someone. That comes from being kind to them. That word is the same one in Romans 2 we have just talked about, meaning usefulness. When we forgive people, we are then able to be useful in their lives. All of this brings us to see them differently than we had first seen them. To do that, we have to see them through the eyes of the Lord. We do that by laying down our souls for them and picking up the soul of the Father. That gives us the kindness, tenderheartedness, and things we need to bring them to the Father and minister to them His way.

All that brings us to the point where we have no bitterness, anger, wrath, tumult, or anything else that is damaging to them or us. *Freedom comes in the process.* This verse started with telling us to let all the bitterness and junk be put away from you. Then we were told how to do it. We have to start with God's grace toward us and let that grace change us. We then have to use that grace toward others so that none of the junk that we have lived through can stick to us and ruin God's plan for our lives.

How?

Now comes the fun part. In this section we are going to explore the wonderful ways the Lord has given us to deal with these issues. They are extremely practical and can be used in any situation and by any person.

The first thing you need to realize is that you have already judged people. That put you into the position of judge over them. The way to get rid of your unforgiveness and judgment is to undo them the way you made them—judicially. You made the judgment as if you were the judge over them in a courtroom, so that is where we need to go to undo them.

What we are going to do now is not what people in new age call guided imagery, nor is it just an exercise in your imagination, even though that is the format that you are going to function in. This is actually real in the spirit realm. What you are going to do is very, very real and will have serious ramifications in your life and the lives of those around you.

Have you ever been in a courtroom? You have at least seen one on TV or in a movie. Go into a courtroom in your mind. The biggest thing for you to see is the bench where the judge sits. It is the focal point of all that transpires in the courtroom.

Get up behind the bench as the judge. It may feel uncomfortable to go there, but you have been there before or else the judgments wouldn't have been made. Each judgment was made when you considered yourself as more important or "over" that other person. What they did to you, you considered worthy of sentencing. They are worthy of death or payment for their sin against you. Your sense of injustice has prevailed and promoted you into the position of judge. You have deemed them worthy of your judgment. That is why you need to start here as the judge.

See the whole scene and understand where you are. You have the authority in this room. What you say goes.

Now call the person who has hurt you to come and stand before your bench. You really should do this verbally, out loud. For example, "I call my father, John Smith, to come and stand before my bench." See him come and stand before you.

Notice what he looks like. In our experience, people see their perpetrator in a variety of ways and it usually means something. If they hurt you a long time ago and are now a lot older, you may see them at the age they were when they hurt you. You have held them in judgment for all this time. Sometimes they will appear to be defiant. Sometimes they are beat up and hurting. No matter how you see them, you need to understand that they are here in your courtroom. This business is very serious and not to be taken lightly. Your life is at stake.

Next, look around and see if Jesus is in the courtroom. Where is He? He is usually standing in the back of the room. This isn't His courtroom. Sometimes He isn't in the room. Either way, you need to ask Him to come and stand next to the defendant. This also needs to be done verbally. If He isn't in the courtroom, you must ask Him to come in. It is very important for Him to be there. The problem has always been that you were doing these judgments without Him and now you must have Him there to set things straight. He is an integral part of the proceedings.

Now get some paper and a pencil or pen. Make sure you have enough paper. Start writing down the charges you have against the defendant. You must have a complete list. Be specific. Some actions will have several charges. For example, let's say you were molested by your father. The charges would include: "you defiled me," "your hurt me," "you stole my childhood from me," "you made me feel like a prostitute," "you ruined my trust," "you didn't love me," "you used me," "you made me feel dirty." There are many, many things involved here. Each one has great meaning and the emotions that go with it. Let the emotions flow. Feel them, let them out. Say what you've always wanted to say about how it hurt you and what it made you feel.

Don't limit it to a certain time frame or event. This is especially true with parents or spouses. Keep going until you feel it is full. You will find you are starting to get redundant and repeat yourself. That is usually an indication that your list is fairly complete.

Now you have everything in place to start the real work. The list is set; the defendant is in place. All charges are understood and written down. Now it is time to turn to Jesus. You only need to ask Him one thing: "Lord, how do you see him?" Let Him show you what He needs you to see about the defendant. This is very important. You are opening up your heart to seeing him as Jesus does. *This is the beginning of laying down your soul for him.* Receive what the Lord shows you. Understand it.

When He is finished showing you what you need to see, it is time to turn to the defendant. You have to say many things to them that will help you do what you need to do here. Each of these sentences are vitally important and must be spoken to him. Let me give them to you in list form so you can follow it exactly.

> Name them (Dad, Tom, Rapist, etc.) I have these
> charges against you.
> To me they are very real.

But I don't have the authority to judge you.
I must turn you over to a higher court with true
authority
To do so I must drop all these charges
Therefore, I declare to you today…
I forgive you for…

Start at the top of the list and read them off. Forgive him for each and every charge that you had against him. Let the emotions flow. Understand that you are releasing him from your judgment. He will have no hold on you anymore. He can't hurt you anymore. You are removing his ability to control you and affect your life.

When you are finished with all the charges, finish it all with the statement; "I declare today that you are totally forgiven from this court." After you say that, bang the gavel. Seal it with the motion that sets things in a court to be known to be accomplished. I suggest that you use your fist on the table or on your leg or something. I have an actual gavel on my ministry table for people to use at this point in the ministry session. I have them bang it on the bible. Something happens in the spirit realm when the gavel is sounded. It is judicially finalized.

After that has soaked in for a moment or two, tell the defendant, "I turn you over to the court of Jesus Christ." Watch what happens. What does Jesus do with him? Many things normally happen. Jesus may hug him. He might put His arm around him and lead him out of your courtroom. No matter what happens, he is no longer in your court and you no longer have to deal with him.

Ask the Lord at this point to forgive you for judging him. You were doing something that wasn't in your authority to do. He told you not to judge and you did. At this point, you need to deal with what you have done and ask for forgiveness. When you ask Him, don't forget to be quiet for a second and let Him speak to you. What did He say to you about forgiveness? Don't leave that place until you hear from Him.

I must put in a word here that is important. When you forgave him, he didn't get away with anything. You took him out of your courtroom and turned him over to the court of Jesus Christ. He has seen everything and it is all recorded. You just put him in the position of having the Lord God of the Universe on the case of justice. God will deal with him in His way. You just put him into His hands and that is final. The benefit is in your life. He no longer has the power to be continually pumping pain into your soul. You are resting in the hands of Jesus and now you are allowing His healing to affect you. It is you getting rid of judgments, not you making someone pay for their crimes. That is up to the other person and the Father Himself.

Don't get into thinking that the sin against you is any bigger than the sin you had in your life. If you stand before God's court totally because of justice, you are in big trouble. It is knowing that, only by the grace of God and the blood of the Lamb, I can stand before Him. I have nothing to brag about and I am not holy based on my own actions.

The beauty of this however, is that the other person is no longer in your court. He has no hold on you. You are free from the judgments and what they were bringing into your life. Now you can actually see him through the eyes of God. You will find that you can even talk to him without animosity and that the pain he has been able to afflict on you is gone. That is a huge benefit.

Self-Judgments

While the kind of pain afflicted by another person can be extreme, one of the most damaging things we do in our lives is to judge ourselves. What makes this so powerful is that we really do know what we've done and there is no excuse that really works. We feel guilty about things and receive lies about ourselves that are next to impossible to eradicate. That is why we must bring things to the God who can do the impossible.

The way we deal with self-judgments is very much like the way we deal with judgments of others. It is still in the courtroom that we have used to make our judgments. However, there are a few differences.

Go into the courtroom in your mind (which is actually real in the spirit realm) and get up behind the bench. This time verbally call yourself, using your full name, to come before the bench. How you see yourself can be very interesting. Many people see a small child come in. That shows they have held themselves in judgment from an early age. If you see yourself as you are currently, then you have judgments against yourself which are current.

Jesus still needs to come and stand next to you, the defendant. You still need to make the list of charges you have against yourself. You know them very well, but it is time to not get defensive or try to justify anything. Just list the charges and don't leave anything out. Let the emotions come and don't deny that you have them. Allow this time to be very open without secrets between you and the Lord.

Don't ask the Lord how He sees the defendant at this point. This will all come out later.

Now is the time to speak to the defendant the same things that were spoken to others you have judged. "I have these charges against you. To me they are very real." Go through all of them each time with each defendant no matter who it is.

Speak out the forgiveness to each charge that is written down. Declare total forgiveness. Bang the gavel and seal it. Turn the defendant over to the court of Jesus Christ. What does He do with them? He usually takes them out of the courtroom. Now things will get very different.

Leave the bench. Go outside the courtroom. Find Jesus and walk up to Him. Start at the top of the list and ask Him, "Lord, will you please forgive me for…?" After each one, listen for what the Lord says to you. Are you forgiven? Wait for an answer after each charge has been read and forgiveness has been requested.

With so many of the charges, you may ask Him what He thinks of the charges. Take for example if the charge was "You are filthy." Ask the Lord what He thinks of that. He will tell you the truth. The truth will set you free from the lie you have believed for so long that you are filthy. Ask Him often about these kinds of charges.

At the end of the list, don't forget to ask Him to forgive you for judging yourself.

This time of dealing with your self-judgments is an intimate and personal time. It is between you and Jesus Christ. Don't try to hide anything from Him. He knows it all already. You are doing what is needed to remove the judgments from your life for you to see yourself the way He does and to live your life in a way that shows the freedom we have in Him.

Forgiving God?

So many of us have a hard time hearing from God or getting close to Him. One of the main reasons for that is because of judgments we have against God Himself. This is so common, it is scary. "Why did God let my Father die?" "Why did God let me be raped?" "Why didn't He stop them from hurting me?" The list of these kinds of statements is very long.

Usually, the problem with these questions is that we don't have the capacity to hear and understand the answer. Most of the time the answer is just because we didn't give God access to the situation for Him to be able to do something about it.

God doesn't stop people from sinning. He tells us not to sin. In the Word He blatantly warns, pleads, convicts, and tells us not to do it. But the choice is always up to us. When has God ever stopped you from sinning? Never! You have always had the choice. When someone who knows Him personally cries out to Him in a situation, He shows up and things happen. Then we have the testimonies of people who were miraculously saved from dire situations. They gave God access and He could act. But the biggest principle to know is that God won't violate a person's will, not even yours. The beautiful thing is that even after a situation is over (and maybe for a long, long time), we can give God access to it and He can bring healing.

The problem in our thinking is that we have to blame someone and since God is in control of everything, we sometimes choose to blame Him for our pain. We know God is all powerful and therefore He should have done something about all the evil that was happening in our lives. Our bad theology is killing us and causing a break between us and the only one who can really help.

There is sin in the world and ever since Adam fell to it, things have been bad. We live in a fallen world and there is great evil out there. If we don't bring God into these situations, we can't expect God to do what He wants to do for us. God has determined that He would limit Himself to not violating our will. On the other hand, He has stated that He will never leave us, nor forsake us (Hebrews 13:5). The difference is whether or not we bring Him into the situation. The key is having a relationship with Him so that we are working with Him and not independently from Him. Then we will have access to learning what His will is and acting in accordance with it.

If we had known all of this to begin with, we wouldn't have made a judgment against God. But since we have judgments against Him, we have to do something about them. Just finding out that God wasn't at fault isn't enough. We have judicially made the judgment that He is guilty and we have to remove the judgment in the same way. It isn't so much that we are releasing God from the sentence of sin, as it is that we have to remove the hindrance between Him and us so our relationship can flow. Our judgments of Him keep Him effectively from working in our lives. It especially hinders our ability to hear from Him. After all, why listen to God if He is just going to mess up our lives even more?

We deal with the judgments against God in practically the same way we deal with the judgments we have against others; we take Him to the courtroom.

Again, go into the courtroom in your mind like you did before and get up behind the bench as the judge. Call the defendant to come stand before your bench. How strange is it to call God to stand before us. It isn't that He is actually guilty, but that we have condemned Him as being guilty. We placed the sentence there and now we have to remove it.

Don't get all hung up on trying to visualize what God looks like. Most of us have to separate God from Jesus because they do different things. Jesus is our friend, but we may feel God the Father is just a tyrant who is there just to condemn us. Remember that Jesus is God and they are one. However, you choose to do it, just put God before your bench.

You don't have to get Jesus to stand next to Him, He is quite capable to stand before you alone.

Then you must list the charges you have against Him and you really must get your emotions into doing it. Cover them all, "You killed my mother! You didn't do things the way I wanted you to do them You didn't answer my prayer like I wanted! You let that person hurt me! You made me angry!" Be thorough. You will find that just listing the charges against Him will make most of them feel empty and unwarranted. When you have the list complete, go through the list of things you must say to the defendant: I have these charges against You. To me they are real. I don't have the authority to judge you, etc. You must state, "I forgive you for..." for each one of the charges. That way your soul knows you have released Him from your judgments and you will have broken the power those charges have in your life to keep you from fellowship with Him.

When you are finished with the whole list of charges, you must ask the Lord to forgive you for judging Him. You've taken the necessary steps in restoring your walk with Him and your ability to hear Him.

CHAPTER FIVE

THE DESTRUCTION OF OFFENSES

In the discussion of relationships, there is probably nothing harder to explain than the area of offenses. There are good offenses and bad offenses. It is good to be offended in some ways and very bad to be offended in other ways. I have seen churches completely destroyed by people who were offended. I have also seen churches destroyed because no one was offended in the right way. What a tangled web to study!

In today's culture, we see people who are offended at so many things that seem to be so petty and not offended at things that should be obviously offending. There are also situations where people are offended at things that are good and shouldn't be offensive to anyone.

How do we sort it all out? There must be a way of understanding that will help us respond in the correct manner. There must be principles in scripture that will guide us through this tangled web.

The Foundation

Understanding the definition of the word is helpful. What is a convicted felon called? An offender. He is one who has gone against the accepted code of behavior and has broken the law. A path had been established that stated certain parameters in our society in such a way that if one gets off that path they are to be punished by the Department of Corrections. They have to pay the price of their offense to society. Their choice of path to walk will have to be corrected so they are on the correct, acceptable path. This analogy of pathways is very helpful in understanding offense.

We all have a path that we have established for our lives. This path is very important to us and has taken a major effort to establish. Our path keeps us moving toward the destination we have determined to be important for survival and acceptance. Our path becomes so important to us that we have considerable fear about getting off of it. We are determined to continue on that path no matter what it costs others. When someone tries to take us off our path, it can become an offense to us. We will fight them with fervor, even to the point of throwing away the relationship with them. Our reason may be, "How dare they do differently than I have laid out! Don't they know how important I am?"

The analogy of pathways works so well because it brings out the power we think we have. When someone offends us and tries to take us off our path, we judge them. They come against our way of living. We then put them in judgment and therefore, they are worthy of sentence. When someone offends us, they become the offender.

If we have the power to judge them, we are therefore God over them. Our path is really self-worship. Our control over our lives is absolute in our way of thinking. How often have you heard someone say, "Don't tell me what to do!" We think we are masters of our pathway. We will determine where we go and who can interact with us. What we want is paramount to anything else and anything that goes against that is offensive and must be rejected. That even includes God Himself. If you don't believe that, just remember the last debate you had with someone else. You came with an opinion and left with the same one: what you think is most important to you.

Why is that a problem? If you have a room of people that all think their opinion is the most important one, there is going to be a lot of strife. It is almost impossible to get anything done with a room of self-worshipping people. Is that the kind of attitude that the Lord can use?

The Definition

In Greek, the word for offense is *skandelizo.* We get our word scandal from it. The definition in the Strong's Exhaustive Concordance is: To scandalize; to entrap, that is, trip up (figuratively to stumble [transitively] or entice to sin, apostasy or displeasure). It comes from the word "skandelon," and it is defined as: A scandal; a trap stick (bent sapling), that is, snare (figuratively the cause of displeasure or sin). Being offended is a trap.

Author and scholar Spiro Zodhiates speaks of these Greek words in his lexicon. He says, "It is the trigger of a trap on which the bait is placed, and which, when touched by the animal, springs and causes it to close causing entrapment. The word and its derivative belong only to biblical and ecclesiastical Greek. In the Septuagint, it answers to the word for *pagis*—trap. However, *pagis* always refers simply to a trap hidden in an ambush and not the results; whereas *skandelon* involves a reference also to the conduct of the person who is thus trapped. *Skandelon* always denotes an enticement to conduct which could ruin the person in question."

These definitions give us great insight into the languages and the passages in the Scripture. To be offended is to be put in the position of eventual ruin. There is a trap that has been set to entrap us and destroy our lives, or at least make us ineffective. The plan of the enemy is to make us think so much of ourselves as to completely dismiss others over petty and insignificant things, keeping us squabbling and bickering and losing the more important things in life.

Proverbs 18:19

An offended brother is worse than a fortified city;
yea, their contentions are like the bars of a castle.

When someone is offended they become like a castle. Initially that sounds really cool to be like a castle, until you really analyze it. He has those walls up because he is trying to defend himself. He has put himself inside a fortress and won't let anyone come close to him.

He will even shoot at people who approach. He hasn't just put others on the outside, but has practically imprisoned himself on the inside. Without interaction from the outside, he is methodically keeping life from coming in. It is an eventual death sentence.

I have been to several castles in England, Latvia, Estonia, and Russia. They all have the same thing in common. There were walls to keep people out and many people died inside and outside. They weren't known for their welcoming atmosphere. They had a message, "Stay away from me or die!"

I have also seen so many people destroy their lives because of offense, so I started looking in the scripture to find out how to help them. There must be a way to get into the castle and help them come to life. The key has been forgiveness on their side and love coming to them from the outside. However, the most important thing is not to become offended in the first place.

The Path

Think of a pathway again. Living in the mountains of Colorado gives me opportunities to wander in the forests. Walking on the pathway is usually a lot easier. Breaking trail is hard work, especially in snow. A pathway is a way to go that is already determined. But what if the path isn't going where you want to go? You have to leave the path and head off on your own. It is really easy to get lost once you leave the pathway. A lot of people get really comfortable walking the same path and it is difficult to get them to try a new one.

It is the same in life. We have ways that we have walked for a long time. Why? Most of the time we don't know, we just know it is the way we've always done it. It is like Tevye, a father whose daughter wants to marry someone other than his choice for her. In the musical *Fiddler On The Roof,* Tevye didn't know why they did what they did, but it was tradition and therefore it was very important. A path that we have walked is somehow important to us. We will stay on that path to the deficit of many other things. We may be offended when someone tries to take us off of our path, and we may offend when we try to take others off of their paths. An offense can be good or bad depending on what path you are on and what path it is taking you to.

Being Offended

We are going to look at this from two different views: being offended and making offenses. Both of them are highly impactful in our lives. The Scripture talks about both of them and how to respond to them. Let's look at some of these.

Matthew 16:21-23

From that time, Jesus began to show to His disciples that it was necessary for Him to go away to Jerusalem, and to suffer many things from the elders and chief priests and scribes, and to be killed, and to be raised on the third day. And having taken Him near, Peter began to rebuke Him, saying, God be gracious to You, Lord; this shall never be to You. But turning He said to Peter, Go behind Me, Satan! You are an offense to Me, for you do not think of the things of God, but the things of men.

Jesus had a path to walk. It was given to Him by the Father God. It was so vastly important. The salvation of the entire human race was in the balance. When Peter tried to talk Jesus into not walking that path, that was an offense to Him. Peter was trying to get Jesus to walk the pathway of selfishness and self-protection instead of sacrificing Himself. To Jesus that was totally offensive. So much so that He even called Peter Satan! Thinking like men think was going to take Him off God's path, and that made Him forceful in His response.

Matthew 18:8-9

And if your hand or your foot offends you, cut it off and throw it from you; it is good for you to enter

*into life lame or maimed, than having two hands
or two feet to be thrown into the everlasting fire.
And if your eye offends you, pluck it out and throw
it from you; for it is good for you to enter into life
one-eyed, than having two eyes to be thrown into
the Hell of fire.*

The "hand" in Scripture signifies what you do. The "eye" signifies what you worship. If what you do is going to take you off the path that God has for you, cut it off and throw it away. If what you are worshipping is taking you off God's path, then pluck it out and throw it away from you. These things are trying to get you off the path and they are causing offense.

If something is going to keep you from God, then living without it isn't much of a sacrifice. It doesn't seem like it at the time, but later it will be one of the best decisions you've ever made. As an example, let's talk about pornography. If pornography is going to hinder your walk with the Lord (and it definitely will!), then cut it out of your life and throw it away. It is better for you to go through life without pornography than to have it in your life and have your family be destroyed by it. If worshipping your heritage in Freemasonry is going to keep you in a life style that is destructive, cut out your focus on it and throw it away. It is better to not have any of it in your life and focus on Jesus than it is to have that in your life.

These are not easy things to get rid of. We really have to want to be free from them. Learning what are true priorities isn't easy and will always cost us. The Lord is continually trying to show us the things in our lives that are depriving us of what He truly wants us to have. There are things that are sucking the life from us and, therefore, are to be cut off and thrown away. Why doesn't God just remove them from us? Because we chose to bring them in and gave them power in our lives. We have to be the ones to see that and choose to get rid of them. As we see how much authority we have given these things, we can make the choice to remove their authority over us and then get rid of them from our lives. It requires that our eyes be enlightened and that we see correctly the influences in our lives.

Matthew 6:22-23

The lamp of the body is the eye. Then if your eye is sound, all your body is light. But if your eye is evil, all your body is dark. If, then, the light in you is darkness, how great is the darkness!

What a wild Scripture! If the eye in Scripture is what you worship, this makes total sense. What is allowed to be the focus of our lives determines the structure of power in our lives. The issue then becomes the focus of our gaze.

If what I am worshipping is darkness, then the one thing that I am pursuing as light is darkness. It then flows through my entire being as I am thinking it is light and the whole time it is darkness. If I am thinking it is light, then how great the power of its darkness is in my life.

If I worship myself, I am thinking my darkness is light and everyone who comes against me is an enemy and must be shut out or eliminated. Anyone who speaks against the path I have laid out for myself (including how I am supposed to be worshipped), will offend me.

Matthew 18:4-7

Then whoever will humble himself as this little child, this one is the greater in the kingdom of Heaven. And whoever will receive one such little child in My name receives Me. But whoever causes one of these little ones believing in Me to offend, it is better for him that a millstone turned by an ass be hung on his neck, and he be sunk in the depth of the sea. Woe to the world from its offenses! It is a necessity for the offenses to come, yet woe to that man through whom the offense comes!

God loves the little children. He makes the analogy that a person who comes to Him must be as a little child in his faith. A child is very humble in the fact that he must rely on those above him. When we are totally dependent on Him, the relationship works. If we are independent, we destroy the relationship. However, if there is a child who believes in our Lord, and is taken off the path, it will be very bad for that person who takes them off that path.

I have seen so many people do this very thing. They have children that are in Sunday School and are learning to walk with Jesus, then they take them and corrupt them into not believing anymore. They show them how to enjoy other things or be distracted by what the world has to offer. They were on the path of growing in Jesus and then, just like that, they aren't interested anymore. Soccer, karate, football, or dance has replaced the glory of the Lord in their lives. Who is to blame? Usually the parents.

This simple scenario looks so innocent and yet is so completely devastating. It is as bad as if they had done the bad things like molestation, abandonment, abuse, and lack of love. All of these take our kids focus off the Lord and makes them think of themselves. We have taught our children that what they want is the most important thing in life, that it is alright to worship themselves.

We think that it takes abject sin to ruin someone, when we have seen how the enemy takes people out with the cares of the world more than anything else.

This passage then tells us it is better for that person to be thrown in the sea with a mill stone around his neck than to take one of these little ones off the path that God has for him. We agree with God when it comes to a child molester, but there are other forms of abuse that we just don't see. Children don't have the personal power to come against this kind of destruction in their lives. They can't see it, but we should be able to.

In the next verse, Jesus says something that is almost outlandish. He said that offenses must come. That is so true. If there is never any choice to leave the path, then we never have the choice to walk in it, we wouldn't need to choose. However, if there is the temptation to leave the path, we have the opportunity to choose the path for ourselves and thereby be much stronger on it. There is a definite sentence against those who cause the offense and they will wish they had never offended a little one off the path of God. How many will be in that group of people? Are we willing to examine ourselves to see if we are of those who have offended a little child to walk away from the path God had for them? May we truly examine and truly repent.

Matthew 13:20-21

And that sown on the stony places is this: the one hearing the Word, and immediately receiving it with joy, but has no root in himself, but is temporary, and tribulation, or persecution occurring because of the Word, he is at once offended.

This passage goes along with the same theme as the last one. This is one of the types of soil spoken about in the parable of the sower. The seed is being thrown onto the stony ground. The seed takes root quickly, but it dies quickly because there is no depth of soil. Jesus tells us what this type of soil is and what this looks like in our lives.

People receive the message of the Gospel with joy, but the reason of coming to Jesus isn't a deep reason. They aren't really believing into Him, just trying to get something from Him or please someone else. When their faith is tested and they don't like the scrutiny or the pressure or they think they are looking bad in someone else's eyes, they fall away. They are taken off the path of God and jump back on their own path. This is being offended in a bad way. They started to change paths to walk the right one, but now they are choosing to go back to the old path of selfishness. They are totally defeated.

What is interesting about this one is that they are offended because of the Word. The Word will expose us and most people are embarrassed and pressured to not stand up for the Word. Most of the persecution we encounter in our culture isn't blatant, but subtle. It is usually just simple pressure to fit in the crowd and not cause waves or not be "one of those" who are different and bringing conviction to people. It is easy to be offended and taken off our path when the peer pressure is on us to perform according to the path others have set for us. Being weak will always bring offense somehow.

Maturity is having depth. When a person is mature, he is not easily shaken. It isn't easy helping people gain maturity. Maturity is happening when a person gets to the point that he isn't offended at what the Word is exposing and doing in his life and the lives of others, and instead is made stronger and more entrenched in what the Word says. Too many times, as I have seen in ministry, people start to grow in the Lord, and the Word exposes problems in their lives, and they run away.

Offenses often take people away from the path the Lord has for them and put them on a path of selfishness and destruction. It always hurts me to see the damage that results from this self-destructive path. It isn't because of someone else, but it is because of the choice they themselves made in their lives that they jump off the path of the Lord for their own. It is the Word of God that exposes that. We will see more of how this works in some of the other passages we are going to explore.

Matthew 15:12

Then coming, the disciples said to Him, You know that hearing the Word, the Pharisees were offended?

The Pharisees were upset because the disciples didn't "wash their hands" before eating bread. This wasn't about germs and hygiene. It was a tradition that you had to dip your hands in water and let it drips off your elbows. It was a ceremonial cleansing, not a physical one. The disciples didn't do this and just started eating. Jesus blasted the Pharisees right where it hurts: their traditions. Their religious legalism was more important to them than the people were. They didn't care who they had to sacrifice as long as they were shown to be righteous in their own eyes.

Jesus told them that they were even more wrong since their traditions were more important than the Word of God. They were willing to give all their time and money to the synagogue and never do anything for their own parents. Jesus was taking them off their path of self-worship and attempting to put them back on the path of the Father. It offended them.

The disciples felt that Jesus didn't understand how highly they were offended and came to tell him as much. People just didn't come up against the Pharisees and yet Jesus did so blatantly and publicly. Was He aware of the social danger He was in? They came to warn Him and wanted Him to take care of it. He didn't.

He explained that He had, in fact, understood. He understood more than the disciples did. They didn't understand the real things that were happening. He wanted to offend the Pharisees from the path of self-worship and get them to see truth. He went on to teach them about what is really defiling and what isn't. Outside isn't the issue, inside is.

So what was the key to offense in this passage? Tradition of men. So many churches have their traditions so firmly in place that they won't receive anything or anyone that does something different than what they have established. What a fight a new pastor is up against if he wants to challenge them in their traditions. "This is the way we've always done it!" they will scream. Woe be to the person who wants to change it.

I have grown up in churches that have had these kinds of traditions. There isn't any scriptural basis for them, but "Aunt Bertha donated that" so there it will stay until Jesus comes. I've seen old, dilapidated pieces of furniture that had a name plate on them "Dedicated in the memory of…" that couldn't be replaced without an entire family getting offended. "We've always sung that song just before communion…" and Gabriel himself couldn't come and play anything else. These traditions are only that: traditions. It sounds like Tevye from *Fiddler On The Roof* again.

In the same story told in Mark, Jesus is quoted as saying, "And you no longer allow him to do anything for his father or mother, making the Word of God of no effect by your tradition which you delivered. And many such like things you do." When our traditions make the Word of God of no effect, then that tradition needs to be done away with.

This is emphasized in **1 Peter 2:7-8**

> *Then to you who believe belongs the preciousness.
> But to disobeying ones, He is the 'Stone which those
> building rejected; this One became the Head of the
> Corner, and a 'Stone-of-stumbling, and a Rock-of-
> offense' to the ones stumbling, being disobedient to
> the Word, to which they were also appointed.*

To those who disobey the Word, who don't think that obedience to the word is important, they will be offended by the Rock-of-offense. Jesus is the Word and to not do what He says to do is going against Him personally. He is the Rock-of-offense. He is called that also in the following passage.

Romans 9:32-33

> *Why? Because it was not of faith, but as of works of
> Law. For they stumbled at the Stone-of stumbling,
> as it has been written, 'Behold, I place in' 'Zion a
> Stone-of-stumbling,' 'and a Rock-of-offense,' 'and
> everyone believing on Him will not be shamed.'*

Most people who are offended are offended because of something incredibly insignificant. When really examined and scrutinized, the logic of it is completely expelled. Then they look stupid in their own eyes or in the eyes of others and they cannot handle looking that bad. They will fight for the justification of their offense not minding what they are truly giving up. What a deep cost for something so insignificant.

These folks will believe that they have been the victims of persecution and are damaged deeply. They really do need to get healed of these offenses and forgive the people who were involved. It is the only way to come out of it with blessings. I've known people who carried these hurts for decades and the bitterness is a fresh as if the offense had happened yesterday afternoon. It is a great pity and their eyes are so blinded to the need for healing. It is very sad and totally unnecessary to carry that burden.

Sometimes the Word offends people when they discover or hear something that is outside of their theology. We all think we have a really good grip on what is in the Word and we put it all in a very neat little pile with all our ducks in a neat little row. What happens when the Word comes alive and shows us things we didn't know before?

In my own life I have had these encounters. The baptism in the Holy Spirit was just one of those times. I had a complete understanding of how those things were supposed to work. I had been raised Baptist and had all my theological ducks in a perfect row that couldn't be rattled. So I thought. I had explained away healing, tongues, prophecy, and all sorts of other things. Then one day the Holy Spirit came crashing into my life and killed all my theological ducks. It was devastating seeing all my dead ducks at my feet. My life was turned upside-down. I tried to run, but His love is faster than I am. To this day I rejoice in what He did that day. He radically changed my theology. Praise God. I have known others, however, that kept their old theology and didn't let God change them. They were offended at the Word and their lives paid the price.

The same thing happened to Jesus and His disciples in John chapter 6. He had a staff of between seventy-two and eighty-four disciples. He had sent them out doing miracles and all sorts of things. Then He told them that they had to drink His blood and eat His flesh. Their traditional theology wouldn't let them accept that. They missed the depth and choked on it. They wanted Jesus to give them physical bread every day. They didn't want to have their selfishness exposed. Verses 60 and 61 say, "Then many of His disciples having heard, they said, This Word is hard; who is able to hear it? But knowing in Himself that His disciples were murmuring about this, Jesus said to them, Does this offend you?" Does this theology take you off the path you have established for yourself?

Verse 66 tells us that many fell away and quit walking after Jesus. They went back to their former lives and lived as if they had never known Jesus at all. Jesus came to the twelve and asked them if they were going to go away, too. Peter said, "Where would we go? You have the words of life." He wasn't able to be offended at the time. He knew where the path of God was and that it was in Jesus Christ, no matter how hard it got. Later, he was confronted with his personal understanding of the Word and what it would cost him. It cost him his selfishness and it was almost more than he could bear. But Jesus didn't leave him floundering and gave him all that he needed to hear. It made him very strong. Praise God he wasn't able to be offended!

Making Offenses

Just like being offended, making offenses has two faces. You can offend people in a good way or you can offend people in a bad way. Making an offense is when you are the one causing someone to get off of his path.

If you are trying to get people off their selfish path, then it is good to offend them. If you are trying to get people off the path of God, then it is bad to offend them. We have responsibility in the actions we do in others' lives.

We have the responsibility to try to help others walk the Christian walk. Our love demands that we are involved in their lives and do what we can to bring them closer to the Lord. Taking their thoughts captive and leading them into the obedience of Jesus Christ is a command in Scripture (2 Corinthians 10:3-5). Paul was continually ministering to people and trying to get them to understand the value of living a life totally sold out to Jesus. He even confronted Peter when he saw that Peter wasn't acting according to the revelation they shared in being set free from Judaism. In Galatians 3, we hear how Paul caught Peter living a lie and even leading others astray. Paul loved Peter enough to confront him and try to get him off the path of Judaism and back on the path of a relationship with God. Peter could have responded incorrectly and become angry and defensive. Instead, he humbly received the word and repented. Paul caused a good offense.

As a minister, I am continually working hard at trying to get people to get off the path of sin and flesh. I have seen the damage that has been done in people's lives and try to spare others from that damage. When we bring that message to them, many people get very upset and angry with us, many of them respond incorrectly and more damage is done. Emotions run high and things are done and said that are regretted later. Because God knew these things, He gave us insight in the scripture about how we are to think in these situations.

There isn't much written about how to offend correctly in those exact words, but there is much about dealing with brothers in sin and how to live. All of that is really about offending people correctly by working to get them off the path of death and destruction.

However, there is a great deal about how to do it in a right way and not offend people by getting them off the path of God. There are warnings about such ways of dealing with people. Let's look at these scriptures.

Romans 14

This entire chapter is about this subject. Paul is showing us that we have responsibility in how we interact with each other and that we don't have the right to condemn each other for thinking differently.

The beginning of this chapter talks about strong and weak brothers. If I were to say that one who is strong eats anything and one who is weak eats only vegetables, it would be a disaster in any room full of people I have ever met. The Word is really clear about this: don't worry about it in someone else's life. It isn't about anyone else in these areas. Each of us must be persuaded in our own minds as to what the Lord wants us to do. If the Lord doesn't want you to eat certain things, then don't eat them. If it is okay to eat things, then don't flaunt it in the face of others. Each of us stands before the Lord, not before each other.

This is very current in today's society and it breaks down usually into two areas: those concerned with physical health and diet and those who are eating religiously.

In every room, there are those who will preach the sin and destruction of unhealthy foods. "Oh dear me! You put a teaspoon of sugar in your tea? You are going to die!" For the most part, healthy eating is very important and we have seen what happens when people don't. However, there are always those who take it to an extreme and condemn anyone who doesn't think the way they do. Give people the information and let them decide. They stand before God just like you do and this issue isn't the biggest issue on the planet. Every month I find a new study that contradicts the study from last month telling us what is healthy and what isn't. Is isn't easy to keep up with what is current. I also find that most things that are deemed healthy are expensive and out of the reach of most common people.

The other area is religious. Lately I have seen many adopting the dietary laws of the Law of Moses in an attempt to be Torah-observant. That is a conviction between them and the Lord, however, many I have known have pushed this on others in a very strong-arm fashion making people think that normal Christians are "second class" and not as spiritual. If the Lord is calling someone to the more Judaic lifestyle, that is between him and the Lord. It isn't to be demanded or enforced. Each one must stand before Jehovah for what they believe is the lifestyle they are called to. What is sin and what isn't is well spelled out in the New Testament and that is the standard by which we must stand.

It is when we condemn others for our own personal convictions that we get into trouble. There are things we are not to compromise on and things that it only matters personally. Sexual sin is always sin and there will always be a stand against it. Whether someone is eating pork or monosodium glutamate isn't.

Then this passage goes on to talk about days and seasons. This is just as controversial as what we eat or don't eat. The Word says that one thinks of a certain day as special and others treat every day the same. The issue is that we are completely convinced that it is what the Lord is doing in us that matters. I will only stand before Jesus for how I treat each day. Do we celebrate Christmas or treat it like any other day of the year? Be convinced in Jesus, live and die for Him and Him only. I take every opportunity I have to bring Jesus into people's lives, and every single holiday, feast, or festival is such an opportunity. However, if I get legalistic about any such day, I will usually offend a younger brother in the Lord and set him up for failure. I must treat him the way that Jesus tells me to treat him and tell him how to live according to the scripture.

The key is whether I judge him as inferior because of the way I determine what is important. He is as important as I am before the Lord. It all boils down to my love for my brothers and the faith I have before God. Right in the middle of this chapter, Paul says this:

Romans 14:13

Then let us no longer judge one another, but rather judge this, not to put a stumbling-block or an offense toward a brother.

I will be held accountable before God for the effect I have in the lives of those I come in contact with. I can take them off the path that God has for them if I treat them in a way that isn't godly. Most of that is just plain attitude. Have I laid down my soul for them? Do I truly love people or do I love my tradition of men more? Do I love myself more than I love the people in my life that Jesus died for?

Romans 14:13-17

I know and am persuaded in the Lord Jesus that nothing by itself is common; except to the one deeming anything to be common, it is common. But if your brother is grieved because of your food, you no longer walk according to love. Do not by your food destroy that one for whom Christ died. Then do not let your good be spoken evil of. For the kingdom of God is not eating and drinking, but righteousness and peace and joy in the Holy Spirit.

Therefore, offending a weaker brother is the prime example of not loving. I can just hear people now saying "Why should I be restricted because they don't know any better?" We who are mature should know better than to sacrifice someone on the altar of our wants or conveniences. People are the most valuable thing on the planet according to God. They were worth giving His son so that they could have relationship with Him. We tend to be willing to throw people away because of what we desire. We should be sensitive to the way we treat people and what we do in front of them.

Romans 14:18-19

For the one serving Christ in these things is pleasing to God, and approved by men. So then let us pursue the things of peace, and the things for building up one another.

Our desire should be to build up our brothers so that they are no longer weaker. We need to protect them and support them until they are older and stronger and able to stand on their own.

Peace between us is the desired result. There is another area of peace we should look for. The peace that rules our lives is the peace of living in Him and letting His peace reign. That is the peace that is worth having. Peace between brothers is an added blessing.

Romans 14:20-23

Do not by your food undo the work of God. Truly, all things are clean, but it is bad to the man who eats through a stumbling-block. It is good not to eat flesh, nor to drink wine, nor anything by which your brother stumbles, or is offended, or is weak. Do you have faith? Have it to yourself before God. Blessed is the one not condemning himself in what he approves. But the one doubting, if he eats, he has been condemned, because it is not of faith; and whatever is not of faith is sin.

It is good not to make my brother stumble. We need to think of the priorities in life according to the values that God determines.

Our sensitivities don't have great value, but our love for our brothers does. It shows the depth of my faith if I can walk in a way as to not damage my brother, but instead build him up. It is an important part of this passage that tells us to not condemn ourselves by what we approve. People are watching us. When we do things that don't seem to damage us but will damage a younger or weaker brother, then those things really do damage us. Our faith will allow us to live without those things if needed. Whatever we do must be done in faith. Faith is trusting in the person of Jesus Christ interacting in our lives.

Romans 14 is quite clear. However, there is another passage that talks about it in another way.

1 Corinthians 8

Paul begins this passage with a reference to food offered to idols. Those with religious tendencies will rock back aghast at the thought of touching anything sacrificed to idols. But Paul states that the idol isn't anything and the sacrifice to it isn't either. We know that there is only one God and that the idols have no power whatsoever. We won't become demonized by eating food that has been offered to idols. People who don't understand the believer's authority and the truth about the realm of demons have great fear about touching things dealing with them.

We know that not everyone grows up and matures as fast as others and that there are weaker brothers watching us all the time. Paul goes into great depth concerning this issue.

1 Corinthians 8:7-13

But the knowledge is not in all; but some being aware of the idol eat as an idolatrous sacrifice until now; and their conscience being weak is defiled. But food will not commend us to God. For neither if we eat do we excel, nor if we do not eat are we lacking. But be careful lest this authority of yours become a cause of stumbling to the weak ones. For if anyone

> *sees you, the one having knowledge, sitting in an idol-temple, will not the weak one's conscience be lifted up so as to eat things sacrificed to idols? And on your knowledge the weak brother will fall, he for whom Christ died. And sinning in this way against your brothers, and wounding their conscience, being weak, you sin against Christ. On account of this, if food offends my brother, I will not at all eat flesh forever, so that I do not offend my brother.*

Paul is adamant about the food not being anything that is harmful, but he emphatically states that our actions could be damaging. He shows us that when we do things that will cause a weaker brother to do something he isn't equipped to handle that we sin by causing that brother to fall by defiling his conscience. The issue is the weaker brother falling. When we aren't careful about those for whom the Lord died, we sin against Christ. Let's look at the scenario as Paul saw it.

In those days, animals were sacrificed to idols in their temples. Bulls were routinely offered in the temple of Diana or Artemas. People would pay big money for a full ox and then the priest would cut its throat and offer the blood. What are you to do with a full-sized ox or bull after the sacrifice? It was dragged out back where they had a butcher shop and steak house. Everyone knew you could buy good meat and eat good steaks in the temple and it was already mostly paid for. The prices were really good. Who wouldn't want good prices for good meat? Sounds really good to me.

Let's say Bruno used to work in the temple of Diana. He is brought to the Lord by an evangelistic outreach and quits his job at the temple. He is young and very excited about his new life in Jesus. As he is walking by the temple one day, he sees you in there chowing down on a luscious steak. What seemed like a real problem to him as a place to stay away from, he now sees you in there really enjoying yourself. As he thinks about it, he is missing the steak he used to have and decides to go back in there for dinner.

While there, he is noticed by the guys and gals who he used to work with. They start giving him a hard time about leaving. Because he isn't strong in his faith yet, he doesn't know how to answer them and is pressured to dabble with them in the services again. He falls and is totally confused and convicted. He feels guilty every time he sees you knowing what he has done and falls away. Because of your ability to eat there without having a problem, he falls. You have lost a brother because of your freedom.

Paul says that because of this he is very careful with his freedom. If it means he won't ever be able to eat a steak again, so be it. His brother is more important than his desire for a steak now and then. At least he won't buy it there.

When I was a youth pastor, my next door neighbor came to me with a small emergency. His refrigerator had failed him and he needed to go buy a new one. Could he put some things in mine while he went shopping for one? I cleared off the middle shelf and he put his things in. I didn't think a thing about it.

As a youth pastor, we had an open door policy. That meant the kids in my youth group could come in our house any time they wanted. The open door was for our house, but they also felt it was the open door of our refrigerator!

One of the kids in our group came by with a friend of his that he had been witnessing to, talking to him of how we lived. As he opened the refrigerator door his friend, noticed the six-pack of beer that was on the middle shelf. He instantly inferred that it was okay to drink beer because the standard of godly living was watching me as the leader of their group. I don't drink. Ever. He didn't know that. My actions told him it was okay.

That night he was asked to go to a kegger. He had too much beer and was in the car that was wrapped around a tree by a drunken driver. How he wasn't killed is a complete mystery to everyone except those who really know the grace of God. It was the message to me that was important.

There isn't anywhere in scripture that says "Thou shalt not drinketh beer." But knowing the damage that is potentially available,

I needed to be more careful, even if it wasn't my beer. My carelessness almost cost a kid's life where a paper sack could have saved it. The Lord was very strong on me to think of what people see in my life and what the cost could be. The warning isn't lost on me.

Taking Up Offenses

Very few things are as devastating as taking up an offense for someone else. When someone hurts someone else, not us, and we get all angry for them, we have taken up an offense. There are great examples in the scripture.

Amnon raped Tamar his half-sister. His offense was against Tamar and her father and protective authority, King David. Tamar went home instead to her brother Absalom. Absalom took up her offense and hated Amnon. Instead of taking him to the God-given authority, his father and king, he took matters in his own hands. His bitterness twisted his way of thinking and he plotted and executed his vengeance on Amnon by having him murdered. His disdain for David was so full that he ended up trying to take over the Kingdom in a military and political coup. It ended badly for Absalom.

When two people enter into a confrontation, they both have the grace to handle it. When someone takes up an offense, he doesn't have the grace for it since it is none of his business. The next chapter covers what he would do with the offense

So much of the deep bitterness that I have seen in peoples' lives is because of taking up offenses that weren't theirs to take up. Forgiveness, getting rid of judgments, laying down our souls, are all principles that supersede taking up an offense.

Summary

Offenses are usually totally destructive. We can very easily implode if we don't pay attention to what is happening in the lives of others, then we will be caught in the trap of offenses and destroyed. Two closing verses wrap up the attitude we need to have so we aren't ruined by offenses.

Psalm 119:165

Great peace is to those who love Your Law, and there is no offense to them.

1 John 2:9-10

The one claiming to be in the light, and hating his brother, is in the darkness until now. The one loving his brother rests in the light, and no offense is in him.

The best attitude to have is to be unable to be offended. If no one can get me off the path, I will always walk in the Spirit. May we pray to be like this in our lives.

CHAPTER SIX

DEALING WITH A BROTHER IN SIN

"There is sin in the camp!" "Do you hear what he did? And he calls himself a Christian!" "That is just too far. We need to just kick him out of the church!"

I have heard all these statements in real life! It seems to be a problem for a church to discover a brother that has fallen into some form of sin. What principles have we already covered in the previous chapters? If we see ourselves as the slave of God, we will serve this brother. If we lay down our soul for him and take up the soul of the Father, we would have nothing but God's view of him. We should be very able to forgive him and have no judgments against him anymore. And by all means we shouldn't allow what he is doing to take us off the path of God in offense. There is so much misunderstanding in this area that I need to cover it here in enough detail to help in the management and administration of dealing with a brother in sin.

How have we done it in the past? My experience has been fairly extensive and I have seen things done in such a wrong manner that the damage to a church and to individuals involved has been quite heavy. I've seen people kicked out of church (in one instance literally). I've seen people slandered and thrown away with no way of reconciliation: "once a sinner, always a sinner." It doesn't seem to matter if the person in question is very well known or an insignificant unknown new one. It has been extremely disgraceful the way people have been treated and all of it done with an air of haughty religiosity and self-righteousness. But the scripture has much to say on the subject. God knew we would need a guide in these murky waters.

Galatians 6:1

Brothers, if a man is overtaken in some deviation, you, the spiritual ones, restore such a one in the spirit of meekness, considering yourself, that you not also be tempted.

First of all, we must see that the brother we are dealing with is a brother. We are not dealing with those who aren't saved. Sinners sin. That is the nature of it all. We can't make sinners behave as if they are saved. They aren't. They do not have the Holy Spirit living in them and everything they do is sin. Sin isn't about actions; it is a condition. A person who has never come to the Lord to have their sins removed will be under that sin continually. Sins are the actions that prove the condition. Sinners sin. Therefore, we must understand this passage is talking about a believer and that makes all the difference in the world.

When Christians sin, it is always a choice. We are no longer under the rule of sin in our spirit. We have the Holy Spirit living within us. We have the capacity to not sin. God wouldn't tell us not to sin if we have the ability to walk free from it. Our spirit is totally saved. Our soul, however, is a whole different matter.

Our soul is made up of our mind, emotions, and will. It is our way of thinking, feeling, and wanting. It is our personality. We interact with others using our soul. There is so much in the scripture about how our soul tries to reign that I wrote about it in my previous book, Truly Loving. Our problem is our soul.

When we sin, it is because we choose to do it. We are operating in our old way of thinking, feeling, and wanting. We are believing lies that we have received about ourselves and what the sin will gain us. If anyone really understood what was happening they would never choose to sin. Therefore, when a person chooses to sin, there is a reason. Finding that reason is paramount to being free from the sin. The reason we haven't responded correctly in the past to people in sin is because we didn't know how to get them set free from it. It was easier to condemn them and make ourselves feel good because we judged ourselves as better than them because we didn't do what they did.

The next part in this passage to look at is the word overtaken. It is the Greek word *prolambano* and it literally means "to be taken in advance." It has the connotation of being surprised or anticipated by something. It could be thought of as if you were running down the street and someone faster than you ran up behind you and overtook you.

Combine that with the next Greek word *paraptoma*. That is the word for deviation in the passage above. It literally means to fall aside, to side slip. The various lexicons have a particularly difficult time nailing down a definition, but mostly they agree that it is something that involves missing the mark and getting off track. The two words together give the idea of a person who side slipped by choosing to walk in a sin and it overtook him. He is now stuck and can't get out on his own. He has believed something that has kept him in the place of defeat and is trapped there.

How many of us have experienced that in our lives? I assume that would be pretty much every one of us in some way, shape, or form. Now is not the time to condemn him but to help him. He might even fight you and try to keep you from helping him. The reasons for that are many and complex. The most important thing we need to realize is that if he doesn't get help, grave destruction is coming his way.

Who can help? This passage calls them the "spiritual ones." Who is that and how do you determine it? Those who choose to walk in the Spirit and not the flesh. How do you determine who that is? By watching their lives and seeing the victory they are living in. It is supposed to be all of us. You are either a spiritual one or you are one overtaken in a fault.

What are the spiritual ones supposed to do for a brother overtaken in a fault? Restore him. It is the Greek word *katartizo*. *Artizo* means to adjust and *kata* means to do so to a fine point. *Katartizo* means to bring it to the fine point of function the way it should be. A good analogy is like reducing a dislocated joint. If someone dislocates his shoulder the function of that shoulder is lost completely and painfully. Then someone comes along and puts the joint back into place as it is supposed to be. It hurts like crazy at the beginning, but feels a lot better almost immediately. Function has been restored and as it heals from the trauma, everything will be back the way it should be.

In this passage, a person's life was taken out of place by sin and the pain and dysfunction is apparent. Someone who knows what to do comes along and helps to set it back in place. It is initially quite painful (emotionally), but very soon the person feels a lot better and function is restored.

This is the focus of the whole verse; the restoration of a person back to the way he should be. True restoration is bringing him back into the relationship he should have with Jesus Christ. Sin always takes away from that relationship and restoration into that relationship is what is important.

The next section is a warning for the spiritual ones who are going to be available to the Lord for helping people be restored. We have to watch out for the warfare that is going to be encountered in this fight for someone's life. We must have a spirit of meekness. What does that mean?

Meekness is one of the most misunderstood words in the scripture. People think meekness is weakness. That couldn't be further from the truth. Meekness is huge strength. My definition of meekness is to be totally submitted to higher authority and empowered by that authority. It means I have no agenda of my own. I only operate in the agenda of the one I am submitted to.

If people are meek, they never have the need to get angry or react to situations. A meek person can be objective in any situation and respond the way God wants him to. That doesn't mean they are just doormats that people can walk all over any way they want to. The meek person has all the authority of the authority he is submitted to. If that authority is God, then he has the full authority that the Lord has in that situation.

Take a policeman for example. As long as he is operating according the rules of those above him, he is the representative of that authority. A Denver policeman is a full representation of the city and county of Denver. It is as if Denver itself is there in the situation. He has full authority to do what he has been commissioned to do. He can arrest someone or even subdue him or her if need be. It isn't the cop who is doing it, but the city of Denver that is doing it. As long as he is operating in submission, he is the full representation.

This strongly applies to the situation of a brother in sin. A person who is going to help him deal with the sin in his life must be totally submitted to the authority that God provides. He must not have an agenda of his own or an "axe to grind" with that brother. He must have the Lord's own attitude and agenda. That is what laying down his soul is all about. Then he will respond correctly and do so in love. He can represent God Himself and bring the healing that is needed.

Part of that is "considering yourself" as it says in our passage. This minister must not look down on the brother he is ministering to. If he considers himself as one who could be in that position, then he won't come into it with condemnation but compassion. We all need to see how susceptible we are to pressures in the world, to sin and think wrongly. We must consider ourselves and our frailty so that our compassion is showing, not our judgment.

That is the temptation it talks about in that verse. We will be tempted to sin as badly as the person we are trying to restore. Our judgment is as bad a sin as anything they did that would cause us to come minister to them. Remember the chapters on forgiveness and judgment and all the scripture we looked at. Our attitude must be straight as we deal with people in sin.

This passage in Galatians 6 is the foundational basis for the rest of our study in this subject. We have to know why we are helping to restore a brother. It must be because of our love for the person who is sinning. It can't be so that we look good to the people who are watching. It can't be for religious reasons. It must be for personal reasons to restore someone back to the fellowship they need to have with Jesus Christ. As we keep this meek attitude in mind, we will respond

DEALING WITH A BROTHER IN SIN

correctly and be able to be used of God to restore a brother and bring healing to a world of pain and damage.

Step by Step Restoration

We are going to look at the most recognized passage concerning this subject. Because people haven't understood this passage, many have done things that are very damaging to others. Let's look at Matthew 18:12-18 in context and with a full understanding of what the outcome is to be.

Beginning at verse 1, we find that Jesus is talking about relationships when He is asked about the Kingdom of Heaven and who is the greatest. Jesus takes a child and uses him as an example. Unless you become as a little child, you can't even enter the Kingdom. He who is the humblest will be the greatest. Then He talks about not offending any of these young ones. We covered that in the last chapter.

Then He tells them that He has come to save the lost. That is the premise of the parable.

Matthew 18:12-13

What do you think? If there be to any man a hundred sheep, and one of them strays away, will he not leave the ninety-nine on the mountains, and having gone he seeks the one having strayed? And if he happens to find it, truly I say to you that he rejoices over it more than over the ninety-nine not having gone astray.

The discussion here is about losing sheep that are valuable to the shepherd. He is seeking the one who has gone astray. He doesn't have to seek the ones that haven't gone astray; they are safe. The one who has gone astray isn't to be shot, condemned, or even punished. The goal is to restore him to safety, to the relationship under the care of the shepherd. The shepherd himself is involved in seeking and gaining back the lost sheep. If that is His attitude, what should ours be?

If we have the same attitude toward people, no matter what they have done, we will be able to be used of the shepherd to restore them to the flock. If we have an agenda, we will be at cross-purposes with what the shepherd has intended. Meekness, therefore, is the most important ingredient in this process. We must be totally submitted to the shepherd's authority and empowered by that authority. Then things will turn out the right way. The very next verse confirms this.

Matthew 18:14

So it is not the will before your Father in Heaven
that one of these little ones should perish.

We must keep this before our eyes constantly to be able to do a restoration ministry to others. It is His will for them to be safe. As it states in 2 Peter 3:9, "The Lord of the promise is not slow, as some deem slowness, but is long-suffering toward us, not having purposed any to perish, but all to come to repentance.

Repentance, therefore, is involved in the process. That is His desire. Sin is killing us and repentance cancels the effect of the sin. He wants us to live and live abundantly. If that is His will for us, it is also His will for the brother in sin.

Matthew 18:15

But if your brother may sin against you, go and
reprove him between you and him alone. If he hears
you, you have gained your brother.

So your brother sins against you. What should you do? Make him pay! Whip him! Hurt him! Make him grovel in the dirt until the pain is completely paid for!

That is the way we have been taught in our society. The problem is that no matter what he does, he can't pay for it. He will never be able to respond enough to make us feel like he is able to be trusted again. God has a better plan. Reprove him between you and him. In other words, go to him and show him what his actions did to you. Work it out between the two of you.

The word reprove is interesting. It is the Greek word *elegcho*. It means to confute him. When I first heard the word confute in the definition of reprove I didn't know what it meant. After looking it up, I gained a favorite word to use. It means to convince beyond all argument, to lay out your evidence in such a way as to win over your opponent so that they have no argument left.

The only way this works is to do it in a manner that will be received. If you go to him full of accusation, the only way he will respond is by defending himself. That doesn't get anything accomplished. It just fosters an argument.

How should you approach it so as not to start another fight? Do your homework first. Go to the Lord and get your healing from the hurt so you have no hurt to be triggered. Lay down your soul and take up the soul of the Father for him. Forgive him and release him from all judgments you have. Find out from the Lord in what area you were wrong.

This way, when you come to him, you aren't trying to get him to pay for your hurts and pains. You will actually have his best interests at heart when you go. You may even be coming to repent before your brother for the things you did wrong. There is nothing like humbling yourself before someone to have them actually receive what you are saying.

The actual reason to go to this brother is because the fellowship between him and the Lord has been breached. This isn't about you getting your payment and making that brother see how badly he hurt you. This is about restoring him. If you are so hurt that you need restoration, then that means you have judgments that keep you from intimacy with Jesus. That makes it your sin and not your brother's. Deal with your stuff privately with your Lord. Then you can start thinking of helping your brother come back to the place he needs to be.

All this is just between you and him alone. No one needs to be involved and you don't have to go talking it up before others. They don't need to take up offenses for you, either.

The hurt comes and you have to respond to it. Take it to the Lord between you and Him first and get everything dealt with there. Then you will have the right attitude to go to your brother alone as a protection for him. That way he doesn't feel threatened and he might have the ability to actually listen to you as you minister to him.

The last part of that verse is the key. If he hears you, you have gained your brother. The goal is gaining your brother back. What a wonderful thing and well worth it. If it works at this level, consider it a huge blessing and go on. How awesome is that?

Matthew 18:16

But if he does not hear, take one or two more with you, 'so that on the mouth of two' or 'three witnesses every word may stand.'

What if he doesn't receive you or your word? What if he responds badly and kicks you out? Now we can beat him! Thrash him! Kick him out! Now we are justified to destroy him! Now we can gang up on him! Right? No.

Now it is time to take it to another level of love. The witnesses you are taking with you aren't there to side with you to convince him of his sin and your righteousness. That is the way I have seen it before. Two or three buddies that are supporting each other, who have probably taken up offenses against this brother, come together to justify their actions and have already judged him as wrong and deserving of sentence. This isn't in compliance with the attitudes that Jesus wants us to have.

What is the role of the people you bring with you? They are to hear both sides and determine how to respond to it. They are there as a loving buffer between the sides. They are there to help both sides come back to the relationship with Jesus. If you take these witnesses and they see that the sin is on your behalf, you will have to repent before your brother and ask his forgiveness. Even if he may be 95% wrong, the 5% you are wrong will require you to ask forgiveness and have it dealt with between you. The 95% should already have been forgiven. The only thing on your mind is to get the sin in this brother's life taken care of and help restore him to the Father.

The witnesses you choose to go with you should be mature people who are willing to go into prayer before the meeting for a period of time and get the heart of the Father for both of you in advance. They are not to be "Yes men" for you to have someone there to agree with you. Submission and meekness are still the order of the day for this ministry. The goal is still the restoration of your brother. If he hears them, you have met your goal and your brother is restored.

Matthew 18:17

But if he fails to hear them, tell it to the assembly.
And if he also fails to hear the assembly, let him be
to you as the nations and the tax collector.

This verse contains two levels. The first one is if your brother fails to hear the witnesses. Now what? Now we can collectively destroy him! We can publicly flog him and drag his sin through the streets of the city! Right? Wrong.

It is time to bring in spiritual authority. Telling it to the assembly isn't about us hanging our dirty spiritual laundry out on the line for all to see. It is about going to those in authority over you and over him and getting their involvement about restoring this brother. You must bring to them the history of all that happened. This is not to make you look good in their eyes, but so they understand the things you have done to humble yourself and go to the Lord. Your concern must be totally your brother. The problem now becomes the effect of the sin in your brother's life and what it might do to others in the church.

He hasn't listened to you after you have done what is necessary to minister to him. He hasn't received the counsel of the witnesses and is setting his heart to be hardened. Leadership needs to know to protect those who are in contact with him and may be wounded or damaged.

It seems that in today's church, people can live in sin pretty openly and still be allowed to have positions of leadership. It seems that leadership doesn't understand personal responsibility to walk in compliance with scripture. Standards have been lowered in so many cases and that is a tragedy. People must be held accountable for the sake of those under them. We have seen too many in leadership fall and damage countless numbers of folks on the way down. Most of that could have been avoided if standards had been in place and accountability was being used. Leadership has lost a lot of its potential because of our lack of true authority where it needs to be.

If he fails to hear the assembly? Finally, we get to condemn him and throw him away! Right? Isn't that what it means to treat him as a Gentile and a tax collector? How has the Lord told us to treat tax collectors and Gentiles? How did He treat them? He loved them and brought to them His message of repentance because the Kingdom of God is at hand.

That is exactly the way we are to treat this brother now. As if he is outside the brotherhood and needs to be brought the message of love again. We know that we are not to have intimate fellowship with unbelievers because they don't have the knowledge they need to for us to closely fellowship with them. We aren't to leave ourselves open to their junk. The same is true about this brother. We are to limit intimate fellowship with him until he repents. We must not have him in leadership over people until his leadership is lined up with the Word of God. The goal is still the same. We love him until he is restored back to the Father.

This is all very tricky when it comes to marriage. A brother in sin could be your spouse. This takes a continual submitting to Jesus in tight relationship as He works on your spouse and your meek and quiet spirit witnesses to him. This is when it is absolutely imperative that you lay down your soul and forgive. Your hope must be in your Lord in ways you have never known possible. He is the God of Hope. You must rest in Him.

It is difficult when it is your children or even your parents. None of this is easy, it is just necessary. If we will walk this out with these principles, we will see miracles like never before. We can see our families restored and that is a great blessing. Don't forget that the shepherd Himself is involved in this process. We are never left without hope. Seek His face and continue on.

Summary

Matthew 18 begins with who is the greatest in the Kingdom and goes into being humble. Then it talks about offenses and the dangers there. It moves into this discussion about how to deal with a brother in sin. After that it talks about forgiveness and the King with the slave and the huge debt that was forgiven and then re-established. This whole chapter is about relationships and how to interact with others. The reality of it, however, is that it started with humility. In our relationships, we need to start with humility. It is our pride that kills us. The sooner we come to that realization, the better off we will be as we encounter other people. Humility isn't an easy thing to do.

CHAPTER SEVEN

SOUL TIES

Is there someone who you can't get out of your thoughts? Every time you think of this person, anger rises up in you or just a sickening feeling in your stomach. You may have been feeling the same emotions for years and you can't seem to be free from them. There just seems to be a link between you and them.

You may not be wrong. There might truly be a link between the two of you. It is called a soul tie and it is very scriptural.

Soul ties are made whenever there is strong emotion or intense activity between two people. Any intense emotion can cause a soul tie: sex, intimacy, bitterness, hatred, abuse, unforgiveness, love, heroics, sacrifice, jealousy, fear, or judgments. We notice them in statements like, "I will never be like my father!" When you tell someone who has said this that they are a lot like their father, he will scream and yell in denial that he is nothing like him, but the evidence is to the contrary.

Our soul is made up of our mind (how we think), our emotions (how we feel), and our will (what we want or desire, how we choose). We have seen it working in every chapter so far. Our soul is our personality, how we relate to other people. It grows and changes as we go through events and situations that happen to us in our lives. We are continually morphing into another person as we respond to the stimuli that occurs every day. We are dealing with how we think and are either changing or making sure we don't change in our thinking processes. Our emotions are in a constant state of flux as we react to the situations we find ourselves in. Our wills are becoming more and more focused on what we really want, whether we admit it or not. When something intense happens between our soul and someone else, it creates a connection between us that causes our focus to be very strong and that connection is the soul tie.

Sex was created to make soul ties. Ephesians 5:22-33 explains it in detail for us as marriage is a picture of Jesus and the church. One flesh is all about intimacy and union God's way. God wanted us to get closer and closer to the person we are married to. Marriage is a covenant. That is the highest commitment known to man. We are in covenant with the Lord also. God wanted to have close communion with individuals and then be involved in the marriage in a high degree. He made it so that when spouses have sex, it would make them closer and closer to each other. Spouses start to think, feel, and want like each other, becoming one flesh. How beautiful!

The real problems come when sex isn't done the way God designed it to be done. When sex is done outside of covenant, very bad things happen. This is called fornication and the scripture is very vocal about that. Fornication robs people of the life they should have. It defiles everything it touches. It destroys people's ability to think clearly, feel correctly, or even have the right kind of desires. It absolutely messes up the soul.

Since sex was made to make a soul tie, illicit sex makes an illicit soul tie. People who have had sex outside of covenant have given parts of themselves to those they had sex with and that part of them is connected to the other person. Since it isnt godly, it is a very negative soul tie. Every ejaculation a man has creates a soul tie. With a woman it is every time she gives herself to someone, or even in a rape situation. Even masturbation over a picture or video of pornography makes a soul tie. That is why the images are impossible to get out of one's head. The only hope a man has is in Jesus Christ. He is the only one who can help get rid of illicit soul ties. We will talk about how to get rid of them later in this chapter.

Sex isn't the only thing that makes soul ties, but it is the most prevalent and is always automatic, functioning without fail. A soul tie with your wife in covenant is a beautiful thing. A sexual soul tie with an illicit partner is a very horrible thing. This shows that soul ties can be good or bad depending on how they were made and why. That is why our discussion about these will be broken up into the two views.

Good Soul Ties

David and Jonathan

One of my favorite stories in all of scripture is the story of David and Jonathan. Jonathan was coming from a much stronger position, being the son of the king. David was coming from a much weaker position, having pretty much nothing. There is evidence to make one think that David was possibly an illegitimate child of Jesse. When asked of Samuel to present his sons, he was shocked that none of them were acceptable before the Lord and didn't even think about bringing in David. He had to be coerced to call David. He was more to him a servant than a son. After David became king, he didn't even acknowledge Jessie and his family as royalty, they were never seen again, but only referred to in genealogies. That makes him a much weaker entity than Jonathan. But Jonathan really loved David, so much that he cut a covenant with him. David didn't have anything to bring to this covenant, Jonathan had it all, a stronger person blessing a weaker person.

Let's look at the scripture about this. 1 Samuel 18:1-3 states, "And it happened, when he finished speaking to Saul, the soul of Jonathan was knit with the soul of David; and Jonathan loved him as his own soul. And Saul took him that day, and would not let him return to his father's house. And Jonathan and David cut a covenant, because he loved him as his own soul."

The language here is very interesting. It says that the soul of Jonathan was knit to the soul of David and that Jonathan loved David as his own soul. That is the picture of what a soul tie is. It is two souls being knit together. There was a definite connection between the two men that was more than just an ordinary friendship. The way they thought, felt, and wanted was blended and connected. They entered into a covenant together that was to last for all life. David could count on it and so could Jonathan.

Even when Jonathan died, the lament of David was intense and deep. Listen to his words as he hears about the death of Jonathan in 2 Samuel 1:25- 26, "How are the mighty fallen in the midst of the battle! Jonathan is slain on your high places! I am distressed over you, my brother Jonathan. You were very delightful to me; your love was wonderful to me, more than the love of women."

I get extremely agitated at people who try to pervert that last line into something homosexual. That comes from people who have never had an actual love for someone else. They try to make love and sex the same thing and that isn't even close to true. These men had a love that most people don't understand. The New Testament talks of this deep love that goes beyond understanding and is totally pure. David was stating that this love was better than anything he had ever known, even from women who were known to have a very emotional capacity for love. This isn't any kind of sexual connotation. I have experienced this kind of love and the very thought of it being defiled by flesh absolutely disgusts me. My love for my wife so greatly exceeds the sexual that it is beyond description.

This soul tie is one of the most beautiful things ever encountered on the planet. This was created by God to show the kind of relationship we are to have with Him. His intention is to have that kind of relationship between Him and us. When it happens between two people, it is something that is very difficult to explain. Intensity of that kind isn't commonly experienced and people try to put it into some form of context they understand. God is love. Love from Him isn't fathomable completely. Anyone who says it is just proves my point. This love is deeply sacrificial and unselfish. Some refer to it as unconditional love. Very few have ever experienced that in reality.

A good soul tie is like that, very hard to explain, especially to people who have never seen it. Bad soul ties are much more common. Good soul ties in marriage are not all that common, but they should be. That brings us to the next category of a good soul tie.

Husband and Wife

Marriage is a covenant. That flies in the face of our culture that teaches us that we can get out of marriages easily and often. A covenant is a commitment for life without exemption. That is a foreign concept to most people, even in the Church, which is a very sad commentary.

God's intention for marriage is to provide a way in the natural for us to understand something in the supernatural. If we can understand the commitment and intimacy of marriage then we will understand the commitment and intimacy between Jesus and His bride, the church. That is the deep meaning of Ephesians 5:22-33.

Because God's intention for marriage is a covenant relationship for the rest of the couple's natural life, everything He designed for marriage will bring the couple closer and closer together, not further apart. Couples are supposed to interact and gain emotional attachment to each other until they are living as one flesh, having their thoughts, emotions, and desires becoming as one. Sex does that. The intimacy of sexual activity is designed to make the couple bond with each other in wonderful and intimate ways.

However, many couples unknowingly defile the workings of their marriage and the resulting interactions between them fall far below God's design for their lives. We have seen this verified through many couples we have observed over the years. They end up making judgments against each other, being angry with each other, and creating a negative soul tie with their own spouse. What was intended to bring them closer was perverted to become a focus of great negative intensity. They hurt each other in deep ways and the damage is vast. They have soul ties, but they aren't good ones.

What was intended is for each of them to lay down their souls for the other and to represent the spiritual aspects of Jesus and the Church, His bride for whom He died. The intimacy God wanted was for husbands and wives to experience the love for another person the way Jesus loves. The beauty of the intimacy He desires to have with us is what He is trying to show us through marriage. When we experience that in the natural, we are closer to understanding it in the spiritual.

My wife and I recently attended a memorial service for the wife of a couple we have known for some time. Their testimony of marriage was something grand to behold. Even their grandchildren spoke it out in stories and testimonies they had of their grandmother. They stated that it is impossible to tell stories of Grandma without Grandpa. They were one. Everyone knew it. They weren't alike in personality or function, but they complimented each other to such a degree that it was wrong to think of one and not the other. They made each other better and without the spouse, it just wasn't the same. They displayed how the whole was more than the sum of the parts. They had good soul ties.

I have found that the experiences my wife and I go through make us closer to each other if we respond to them correctly. Adversity gives us the opportunity to find the Lord in it. We wouldn't know God as we do if we hadn't gone through the times of trouble. It is the tribulation in our lives that build the emotional ties between us. The more intense the situations, the greater the soul ties we have. We know that if everything else goes wrong, we will have each other's love. We are a lot closer now than we have ever been and that is a great blessing.

One of the greatest joys we have is to show other couples how to respond correctly and build their lives together. As we show them how to get rid of the judgments and how to lay down their souls, we have the privilege to see God heal marriages and couples get closer and closer to each other and to the Lord. These are good soul ties and we are praising God for them.

Our Covenant with Jesus

The goal of our marriage is for us to become even closer to the Lord Jesus Christ. Our soul was made to have fellowship with God in the first place. When things are working the way they were first designed to, we will have deep, intimate relationship with our Lord. That is what He had with Adam in the beginning. The fall took that from us and built a barrier between God and man. Redemption buys us back from sin and death and restores our relationship. That is what our Christianity is all about!

The Father God has desired fellowship with us and that is why He created us in the first place. Redemption is the way to bring us back to that purpose.

We see the example of David in the Psalms as he cries out for that intimacy in relationship. One of my absolute favorites is Psalm 103. The first 2 verses state this:

"Bless Jehovah, O my soul, and all within me, bless His holy name. Bless Jehovah, O my soul, and forget not all His benefits;"

When all that is within me is blessing Him, that is true intimacy. When my soul is attached to him in this kind of personal way, I start to think like Him, feel the way He does, and desire the things He desires. The goal of Christian maturity is to become more and more like Him in all that I do and think. That is becoming Christ like. That is the ultimate soul tie.

Jesus prayed that very thing for the disciples and ultimately for us in John 17. Look at verses 21- 23:

"that all may be one, as You are in Me, Father, and I in You, that they also may be one in Us, that the world may believe that You sent Me. And I have given them the glory which You have given Me, that they may be one, as We are One: I in them, and You in Me, that they may be perfected in one; and that the world may know that You sent Me and loved them, even as You loved Me."

Being one with Jesus and the Father as they are one is a mystery for the ages. What a wonderful thing that we have yet to experience fully in our souls. It is true about us in the Spirit, but our souls are still in the fight over lust and love. We are still trying to rule our own lives and not let Him reign. We are trying to let our soul be god. As we yield to Him and get rid of our hardness of heart, we find a closer communion with Him and find that our souls are becoming more and more like Him. Our submission is accomplishing something our independence couldn't. We are blessed when our souls start becoming closer and closer to Him and we think, feel and want like He does.

As we discussed in chapter 3, the greatest thing we can do is lay down our souls. As we lay down our souls and take up the soul of the Father, it is obvious that we are gaining good spiritual soul ties. If we truly love someone else, we are expressing God's mind, will and emotions for that person. We will form good soul ties as we represent the soul of the Father. Likewise, when we pray for someone else, we gain the heart of the Father for them.

However, when we misuse our bodies after becoming believers in Jesus Christ, some very adverse things happen that we should be made aware of. Look at 1 Corinthians 6:11-20.

> All things are lawful to me, but not all things profit. All things are lawful to me, but I will not be ruled by any. Foods for the belly, and the belly for foods, but God will destroy both this and these. But the body is not for fornication, but for the Lord, and the Lord for the body. And God both raised up the Lord, and He will raise us up through His power. Do you not know that your bodies are members of Christ? Then taking the members of Christ, shall I make them members of a harlot? Let it not be! Or do you not know that he being joined to a harlot is one body? For He says, "The two shall be into one flesh." But the one being joined to the Lord is one spirit. Flee fornication. Every sin which a man may do is outside the body, but he doing fornication sins against his own body. Or do you not know that your body is a sanctuary of the Holy Spirit in you, which you have from God, and you are not of yourselves?

*You were bought with a price; then glorify God in
your body, and in your spirit, which are of God.*

When we sin sexually without bodies, we are actually making the Lord have sex against His will since it is His body we are using. Our tie with the Lord is much closer than we typically acknowledge. Since He and I are both inhabiting the same body, our souls have the opportunity to be one in very intimate ways. Will we let Him be part of our most inward thoughts and emotions or will we try to block Him out? He already knows them all. As we acknowledge Him and purposely open our thoughts and emotions to Him, we receive His thoughts and emotions. As He changes us, our soul ties with Him can be much more intimate than we have ever believed possible. This is what He is calling us to.

Bad Soul Ties

Here are some biblical examples of bad soul ties and how they functioned. God has recorded some very interesting stories in order for us to learn. As I studied these, it became apparent to me that I "knew" these people I have seen the principles and consequences in the lives of people I have known.

Shechem

In Genesis 34, we read the story of Jacob and his sons as they first are establishing themselves in the land after the encounter with Esau. They went to the valley between Mt. Gerizim and Mt. Ebal where the blessing and the curses were spoken by the children of Israel when they came into the land after the wandering years in the wilderness.

They bought some land from the Head of the city there, Hamor, and his son Shechem. Dinah, the only daughter of Jacob, was tired of having only boys around and went to meet the daughters of the land. While there, she was seen by Shechem and he lusted after her in the worst way. He raped her.

Verse 3 states that his soul clung to her. He couldn't think of anything but having her as his wife. He gained a soul tie that was obsessive and all-consuming. It was so bad that he pleaded with his father, Hamor, to get her for him as a wife. They went and met with Jacob and her brothers. The scriptures say that Shechem was more honorable than any of the house of Hamor (and he raped Dinah! What does that say about the rest of them?) and wanted to do everything he could to make up for his sin against her. He offered them any bride price they named. They rejected him.

Jacob and her brothers told them that they couldn't allow a marriage because Shechem was uncircumcised. Shechem proved himself to be one of the greatest salesmen in history! He went to the men of the city and convinced them all to be circumcised!

Then the next principle of soul ties comes to bear. Dinah's full brothers, Simeon and Levi, gained bad soul ties against Shechem through judgment and hate. They waited three days until all the men were in considerable pain from the circumcision and went into the city with swords killing all the men including Hamor and Shechem. Because of this, Jacob didn't bless them at the end of his life, but cursed them. Bad soul ties have no benefit and even though they had killed the one responsible for Dinah's rape, they were guilty of murder of all the other men. There was nothing Shechem could have done to make up for the crime he committed. Soul ties are destructive.

Potiphar's wife

Joseph was taken to Egypt as a slave, sold by his brothers. In Genesis 39, we are told the story of what happened to him there. He was purchased by a man named Potiphar. Looking at the scant amount of evidence in the scripture, the best we can determine is that Potiphar was the captain of the executioners for Pharaoh. It also says he was a eunuch. The chances are that even though he was a eunuch he wanted the companionship of a woman and got married. She would be precious to Potiphar, but unfulfilled sexually. Joseph was in a tough situation. He was handsome and appealing. He was also full of integrity and wouldn't go against what he knew was Godly.

Joseph was influential as the head of the household. He was available as he was always around the house to take care of the things of his master. Potiphar's wife lusted after Joseph. He continually said no to her. Her fantasy of having Joseph gave her a focus on him that was obsessive. His rejection only made her want him more. She finally saw her opportunity and tried to seduce him, even grabbing him physically. He ran and left his coat behind in her grasp. She was rejected! There was evidence of what she had tried to do and the only recourse she had was to turn it around and accuse Joseph of trying to rape her. He was wrongfully sent to prison for it.

The principles here are interesting. She focused on Joseph. The more she thought about him, the deeper she went emotionally. She had developed a soul tie with him that he didn't share, nor did he want. It drove her to the point of actually physically accosting him. It cost her everything she had obsessed over.

Samson

Samson's life is recorded in Judges 13-16. Samson wasn't exactly the most godly hero of the Bible. He was used of God, but didn't show much godliness. The only time we know that he prayed was at the end of his life. However, he was a manly man, and had a real problem with lust. Women were his downfall.

His first wife was a Philistine woman who really pleased him. He gained such a focus on her that it ended up costing the Philistines the lives of thirty men. Her father gave her to one of Samson's closest friends (such friendship!). He wanted to give him her little sister and Samson burned all their fields. They burned her and her father. So far none of this was working well for Samson even though it was all planned by God to mess with the Philistines.

Then he had a tryst with a harlot, still getting involved with the wrong women and his focus just made him an angry man that had the power from God to do something about it. Then he met Delilah.

His focus on her was so strong that he lost all reason. He couldn't see how she was baiting him and setting him up for a fall. Soul ties will do that to you. He finally told her the real secret to his strength, the final breaking of the Nazarite vows he had lived under all his life. His strength wasn't in his hair, but in the vow to be set aside for God's use only.

His soul ties led him to the final destruction of his life. He was a broken man with no sight and no future. I have always wondered what he could have done if he had put his focus on the Lord instead of women. That is something for all of us to think about. What could we do for the Lord if we got rid of all our soul ties?

Saul and David

One of the most famous soul ties is the one King Saul had with David, starting in 1 Samuel 18. David was an innocent bystander. Saul had a major problem.

Immediately following David killing Goliath, Saul turned sour. He was mighty impressed with David on the battle ground. His courage, demeanor, faith, and godliness were undeniable and highly commendable. His victory sealed it and Saul told David that he was to come live in the King's house. Word got out of David's victory, as exploits like that are hard to keep quiet, and the imagination of the people had been captured. As they entered into the city, the women sang, "Saul has slain his thousands and David his tens of thousands!" It burned Saul that they had attributed more to David than to him. Jealousy entered in and Saul couldn't think of anything else. David had become his negative focus.

Saul tried to pin David to the wall a couple of times with a spear while David was playing his lyre. David had to play because of the evil spirit on Saul that tormented him on occasion. Saul knew that Jehovah had left him and was with David. The jealousy was too great for his mind and he planned murder against David. He even went so far as to use his army to try to find David and bring him down. God continually protected David and he became a mighty man of war and valor.

Saul gained a soul tie because of his own guilt of running away from God and seeing God's favor on someone else. Whenever someone becomes the pointed focus of our lives, we will gain a soul tie with them. They will inadvertently become a twisted form of a god to us and they will rule our lives without even being involved! Hatred will almost always make a soul tie.

Amnon and Tamar

Probably the most dramatic illustration of the depth of soul ties is the story of Amnon, one of the sons of David. In 2 Samuel 13, Amnon lusted over his half-sister Tamar, the full sister of Absalom. He wanted her so badly, it made him sickly every morning to the point of being noticed by his cousin Jonadab. Amnon knew she was a virgin and that bothered him because it precluded him doing anything with her.

Jonadab was a very intelligent guy, some would say sneaky. He told Amnon of a plan to get Tamar into close proximity to him. It doesn't say he told Amnon to rape her, it was only to get her close to him. Amnon took it to the extreme. He lied to the King about being sick and asked for Tamar to come to his chambers to feed him. This was all legal and safe with the servants there. She came and made lunch for him. He went into the inner chamber where his bed was and asked her to come in there. Then he sent away the servants and raped her.

She then pleaded with him to ask the King, their father, for permission to marry her. Amnon refused, as his self-focus was so strong that he wouldn't be reasoned with.

Then something happened that is so often true with soul ties, especially sexual ones. The Bible tells us that Amnon hated her with a hatred that was greater than the lust he had for her before. He hated her so much that he kicked her out of his chambers still naked. She was even more humiliated and ran to her brother Absalom's house. He saw and verified that she had been raped by Amnon and told her to keep silent. She lived desolate in Absalom's house for the rest of the story.

David was either not informed at the time, or he chose to do nothing about it. Absalom was never submitted to David. Absalom picked up Tamar's offence and hated Amnon. Two years later, he killed Amnon at a feast. David knew enough of Absalom's character to think he had killed all his sons. Jonadab was with the King when the news was presented and told him that only Amnon had been killed and it was because he had raped Absalom's sister. Absalom fled and later returned to usurp David's kingdom and eventually be killed in the fight that developed.

Everyone in this story was greatly damaged. Amnon had a lustful soul tie with Tamar that turned into a hatred soul tie after sex. His life was destroyed. There was no godliness in him. Tamar's life was devastated and her identity was always that of the one who was raped. Absalom had a hatred soul tie with Amnon and then with David. David was the King and did nothing about all the sin that was happening in his house. All this came about because David had a lust soul tie with Bathsheba in the first place that ended with David murdering her husband and the baby dying.

This story strongly illustrates the power of soul ties and what they can do to a life, a family, a kingdom, and a society.

Judgments

As we had covered before in the chapter on judgments, when we judge someone else, we end up being judged the same way by ourselves, others, and God. When we have judgments against people, our focus is strongly on them. It knits our soul to them and they own our lives without necessarily being involved with us. They may not even know of our judgments against them. Matthew 7:1-5 and Romans 2:1-11 are very plain about the effects of making judgments. Judgments are made from the soul and cause us to focus on someone inordinately. That makes a soul tie.

Sex

Several of the previous biblical examples of bad soul ties were a result of sexual sin. God invented sex. It is intended to show us the relationship between Jesus and the Church, His bride. In the beauty of marriage, intimacy is to be a beautiful thing that enhances the oneness that should be experienced in the covenant between a man and a woman. The promise of marriage is one of the first things that God intended. It says in Genesis 2:24:

> *Therefore, a man shall leave his father and his mother, and shall cleave to his wife and they shall become one flesh.*

God wanted to show the intimacy of covenant relationship and invented sex for that purpose. When a couple consummates the marriage it starts a soul tie that is intended to bring them closer and closer together. The longer the couple is together, the greater their connection. It even works for unbelievers. Marriage is a wonderful thing.

When sex is done contrary to the way God intended it, there are dire consequences. The scripture is very clear about sexual sin.

Inordinate sex produces inordinate soul ties. Every form of sexual sin works in this same way. All sex done outside of the covenant of marriage is called fornication. That includes adultery, homosexuality, masturbation, pornography, voyeurism, incest, bestiality, or any other perverted sexual function. Sex is to be between a man and a woman under the power of covenantal marriage. Period.

Every soul tie made through sex outside of covenant is to be broken for healing and freedom to be obtained. Each soul tie must be broken individually. They can't be broken in groups. They were made individually and must be broken the same way.

For sexual soul ties, there must be forgiveness first. You must forgive the people you had sex with and you must forgive yourself for having sex. You can review the chapters on judgments and forgiveness if you need help in that area.

When people have sex, they give some of their soul to the other person and take some of the other person's soul in exchange. When this is done for a long time and many repeated times, the soul gets hollow and feels empty. Those parts must be taken back and given back. This is especially true with sexual soul ties.

Breaking Soul Ties

What good is it to tell people about soul ties and not tell them what to do about them? There are several principles that need to be done to break a soul tie. They are all important and none of them are necessarily easy or comfortable to do. If you don't like doing a part and try to skip it, the healing and freedom won't be as great as you would like them to be. Please, be thorough. Save a lot of heartache down the road and deal with everything now.

1. Confess you have it

Denial is one of the greatest weapons against healing. Finally admitting that you have a soul tie is very important. Bringing it to the Lord is even more important.

Admitting to Him how you established the soul tie begins the freedom process. Confession is the way to open the door. "Lord, I did have sex with her. It was my fault and I was wrong. Will you please forgive me?" "Lord, I have hated him for a long time and my hatred is killing me. I am so wrong to be like this. Will you please forgive me?"

Whatever sin it was that opened the door to this soul tie must be confessed. When you take responsibility for your actions, then, and only then, will you be able to take it to the Lord in repentance. Don't try to justify it. Just admit it and take ownership of the sin. See that it is against what God would have in your life. Understand the damage that it has caused in your life and in the life of others around you.

You must ask for forgiveness from Him. That is the only way to deal with this sin. You can't pay for it any other way. It is only His blood that takes away sin. Ask Him.

What did He say? Don't forget to actually listen and hear Him. Did He forgive you? Stay until you know.

You may have to forgive yourself. If you don't feel that you deserve to be forgiven, you may not allow yourself to hear that He has forgiven you. Let yourself receive forgiveness by forgiving your-self. His blood washes it all. Your sin isn't greater than His blood.

When you know you are walking with Jesus through it all, you know you will gain the freedom. That is what He does! And He is the only one who can free you!

2. Ask to see them correctly

Ask the Lord to show you how He sees the other person. It doesn't matter how you obtained the soul tie, it was because you had a flawed view of them. When you see them the way the Lord does, you will be able to deal with what happened. If you will lay down your soul for them, then your soul will be able to be restored.

Love breaks the power of lust every time. If you see them the way the Lord does, you will not lust after them anymore. If you truly love them, you won't hate them anymore. Even if what they did to you was truly wrong, you can leave that with the Lord as you see them His way. This is how you are going to be able to live without having that other person own a part of your life. You must be free.

3. Forgive them

It is essential that you forgive them and release them from all judgments you have against them. Part of the reason you have a soul tie is because of the judgments. As you forgive them, you will be able to think of them without holding them to their past. You will be able to respond in Jesus.

You may also have to ask for forgiveness. The chances are very good that you were both participating in the sin that caused the soul tie. If you sinned against them, then you must ask for forgiveness and build reconciliation. Only ask forgiveness for the parts you were truly wrong in. Don't bring up anything else or try to justify your actions. Just admit you're wrong and ask him or her to forgive you. It is that simple, but it isn't easy. This is how you are going to find freedom for your soul.

4. Turn that person over to the Lord

To get them out of your hands and into the hands of Jesus, you must actually state that to Him. "I turn (person's name) over to you, Jesus. I give him to you so that I don't have him in my hands anymore."

After forgiving the person and releasing him or her from the sin and judgments, you now need to give the person up to Him so He can deal with him or her without your interference.

5. Renounce the open door

To renounce something means to take away its power to affect you anymore. You had submitted to the authority of it when you did whatever it was that brought in the soul tie. Now you are taking away its authority so it can't work in your life anymore.

It will look something like this. "I renounce fornication in my life. Fornication, you no longer have authority in my life. Jesus has forgiven me. I have forgiven myself and now you no longer have any authority in my life."

6. Break the soul tie verbally

Now it must be stated by you verbally and with authority that the soul tie is broken and cannot remain effective.

"I now break this soul tie. It no longer has a hold in my life and can no longer affect me. I take back all parts I gave away and I give back all that I took from them. All evil or wrong connections are hereby severed and made of no effect."

7. Thank the Lord.

As with all things that we do with Him, thanksgiving is always warranted. That is how the deal is sealed. This is our acknowledgment to God that He freed us and He gets the glory! Thanksgiving is totally relational and personal. It is the icing on the cake.

Don't Make Any More!

As you can see with the importance of soul ties, you don't need to make any new ones! Don't do the sins that you did before that caused them! Do what the Lord is wanting you to do. Walk with Him. The soul ties you will make with Him in control are good ones.

Forgive everyone every time and do it quickly. Love your enemies and pray for those who despitefully use you (Matthew 5:38-44).

Lay down your soul for people and you will find your soul will remain healthy. Trust the Lord and not the arm of flesh (Jeremiah 17:5-8).

Stay away from every form of fornication. It is amazing how the things God tells us to do or not to do are for our good!

CHAPTER EIGHT

SEXUAL PROPRIETY

A book on relationships would be incomplete if it didn't talk about male/female relationships. The problem here is that there is too much to cover. This is a subject for another entire book. Reading the scripture is the best way to gain understanding in this area. I am not going to attempt to cover everything in this chapter, but I am going to lay down some principles and observations.

I have been ministering to men for the last decade about the issues of pornography and sexual perversion. My observations are not just passing and unrelated. They are based on hard involvement in people's lives and the damage done by not doing things the way God wanted them to be done. In our one-on-one healing ministry, we have dealt with couples and both male and female individuals. The intense damage and suffering people have gone through because of lack of understanding in this area has become the reason for presenting this material. I hope you will be open to hearing some of the things we need to say in this chapter.

Why Sex?

As we have discussed in previous chapters, God had a purpose behind inventing sex. It wasn't just thrown in because He couldn't think of another way to make babies. He had a purpose and a plan. He also knew the power for misuse. He wanted mankind to experience things that would enhance their lives and their relationship with God. Nothing was created without a plan in mind and a way of expressing oneself through what was created. Sex has purposes and we can express ourselves through it. There are reasons why it is so powerful. Because it is so powerful, it can and has been so severely perverted.

Ephesians 5:21-33

...having been subject to one another in the fear of God. lN'ives, subject yourselves to your own husbands, as to the Lord, because a husband is head of the wife, as also Christ is Head of the assembly, and He is the Savior of the body. But even as the assembly is subject to Christ, so also the wives to their own husbands in everything. Husbands, love your wives, even as Christ also loved the assembly and gave Himself up on its behalf, that He might sanctify it, cleansing it by the washing of the water in the Word, that He might present it to Himself as the glorious assembly, not having spot or wrinkle, or any such things, but that it be holy and without blemish.

So, husbands ought to love their wives as their own bodies, (he loving his wife loves himself), for then no one hated his own flesh, but nourishes and cherishes it, even as also the Lord the assembly. For we are members of His body, of His flesh, and of His bones. "For this, a man shall leave his father and mother, and shall be joined to his wife, and the two shall be one flesh." The mystery is great, but I speak as to Christ and as to the assembly. However, you also, everyone, let each one love his wife as himself, and the wife, that she give deference to the husband.

There is so much in this passage that it makes it difficult to extract all we need from it. The biggest thing is that God invented marriage for us in the natural so we could understand in the super-natural the awesome relationship we have as the bride of Christ to our Lord and Savior. That relationship is the greatest relationship a person can experience. So God gave us marriage for us to learn how to interact in a close personal commitment with another person here so we could start to learn how to have the interaction we need with Jesus. No wonder marriage has been attacked so strongly in our culture.

When God talks about sex, He does so only in the context of marriage. Any sexual activity outside of the covenant of marriage is called fornication and is strictly forbidden. We need to extend the principles here to understand why.

What is the most intimate thing between husband and wife? It is called sex. What is the most intimate thing between Jesus and the church? It is called worship. God gave us the intimacy of complete openness and exposure in acceptance and giving so we could begin to understand a little of what true intimacy with the Lord is in worship.

So few have had the intense intimacy during worship. The reason is because we have given up true intimacy by having what was intended for only one person to be shared with many. If it is acceptable for a person to have multiple sexual partners, then the personal intimacy of having sex with only one person for our entire lives is lost completely. Our worship is not to be shared with many gods or idols. It is intended for only one person forever. So is sex.

People mock folks who say they are waiting for marriage or that they are saving themselves for their future husband or wife. Such is the depth of defilement we are living in right now. The beauty of the perfect intimacy is so far beyond the understanding of those who are already defiled as to be totally incomprehensible.

So rare is the understanding that I am considered the weirdo when I go to teach young people on relationships. Their mouths drop open with a wide-eyed expression as they actually ask me, "Are you kidding me?" "Nobody thinks that way anymore!" "We are living in the modern age; no one expects that of us any more!"

God is serious about this. He knows the implications and consequences of missing the principles when we go against the Word of

God. I have never seen it fail. When people go against God's way of doing sex, they pay dearly. Every time. No matter who, no matter the circumstances, no matter why. The pain is very real. That is why I feel we need to talk about sex and not just shove it under the rug and let people learn it the way the enemy wants them to.

To the Men

I am pretty mean to guys when talking to them about how to treat the women. Men are stimulated visually initially. What they see is crucial. The problem is, they are always looking to see what they can see. In today's society, that is pretty much everything. There isn't anything held back. They can see just about anything they ever wanted to just by going to the mall!

It takes a real man to be a godly, pure man. If you try to get away with anything, you will and won't. You will have the sexual fun you are looking for, but it won't mean to you what you think it will mean. The cost to your soul is enormous. Men are called to be the priests in the church. You represent Christ, our High Priest. What you do to others is vastly important and you can't be having sex with them and thinking they are important to you. You just used them. There is no real concern for them and I can prove it.

Lust takes from others for your "benefit" no matter what it costs them. Love gives to others for their real benefit, no matter what it costs you. You can't lust and love at the same time, they are diametrically opposed. You can't love someone and still want to look at her body or touch her. To want to touch her or even look at her body is lust. Love is the real key to breaking the power of lust. Do you truly love her? Have you laid down your soul for her? Do you see her the way the Father sees her? What does He desire for her? Do you really think that God wants you to touch her, look at her body or lust after her? I don't think so.

When you see her God's way, you will want to protect her, not hurt her. You will want the absolute best for her. When you lust after her you are actually offering her on the altar before your god, which is you. When the offering is done, she will mean very little to you. Real concern for her means you won't touch her inappropriately. Your real desire for her is to have a relationship with the Lord and walk in the purity and innocence of a loved daughter and holy bride. Everything else is damaging.

Men live in fantasy realms. Your mind is mostly unhindered from anything you want to think about. You think about being the hero and being the best fighter or warrior or whatever it is that you care about seeing yourself like. When it comes to women, you are loved, accepted, the best and nothing is withheld from you. The women in your fantasy will do anything you want and will always accept you no matter what. You really think that you are alone in your thoughts, that you can get away with anything. Not true.

Psalms 139:1-2; 23-24

O Jehovah, You have searched me and known me. You know my sitting down, and my rising up; You understand my thought from afar off.

Search me, O God, and know my heart; try me, and know my thoughts; and see if any wicked way is in me; and lead me in the way everlasting.

The Lord knows every thought. He knows them so well He can pick them out of a crowd at a distance! He knows what you want and how you want it. He knows what you are thinking about the girl you are talking to and what you are trying to do. He also knows the girl you are talking to and loves her with the same love He loves you with. He knows which movies you watch and what you are thinking when you see the women on the screen and what you think about later in the privacy of your own bedroom. He knows what porn you've seen and He actually knows each of the porn stars personally and intimately. He loves them and having men lust after them and doing all the things men do over them isn't His plan.

We have left God out of our personal lives to the point where we don't know His intimate conversation with us. We don't really care what our thoughts and actions are doing to the people around us. If we did, we wouldn't be doing or thinking these things.

It is up to the men to act godly. We have to be the protectors God intended us to be. The women around us should be the most secure and protected women on the planet. If a man doesn't want to do things God's way, it won't matter what I have to say to him. This book won't change his mind if he doesn't want to do what God wants to do. We really do know what God wants. It is time to be honest and submit to Him.

Principles for the Men

1. Integrity

Walk a walk with Jesus that affects your every action and thought. Practice the presence of Jesus as if He were standing right beside you, because He is. Have the courage to stand up and be the man you are supposed to be. It isn't just sexually, but in every way. You are not doing this because of the law, but because of your relationship with Jesus Christ and it is for love for Him that we do what we do.

2. Get rid of the past

Get alone with Jesus and talk to Him about what you have done sexually in your past. Confess what you have done. Ask His forgiveness. Hear from Him that you are forgiven. Forgive yourself.

There are so many things that you need to do, but the biggest is to bring it all to Him and let Him walk you through all the things you need to do. Get in touch with this ministry and get the DVDs of the Pure Man Conference and that will bring you all the tools you need for walking in freedom sexually. www.Puremanconference.com.

3. Don't touch a woman

In 1 Corinthians 7:1 it states, "But concerning what you wrote to me, it is good for a man not to touch a woman"

It means just that. It is good for a man not to touch a woman. We have become too familiar with women and touch them in ways that aren't appropriate but nobody notices anymore. We physically joke around and it doesn't seem to matter to anyone, except you know you've done it. It is simple—don't touch them.

Even in church, we hug women and most of the time it isn't the right kind of hugging. I don't allow a woman to hug me straight on. Most men don't seem to mind. I wonder why? I call those kinds of hugs "boob crushers." I don't need to feel a woman's breasts on any part of my body. I don't want anyone feeling my daughter's breast on their stomach. Be careful. You know what is right.

What you see with your eyes, you have touched with your mind. Since men are stimulated by sight, it matters what you look at and how you see it. When I walk around in the mall, I can't help but see what I really don't want to, but it is the thoughts I have about it that make it or break it. My constant conversation with Jesus is what makes it pure. He shows me what I need to see and none of the sexual stuff is appealing. I need to love them, not lust them. Jesus and I do this together.

4. Accountability

Most ministries that deal with pornography use accountability as the highest form of freedom to offer. It doesn't work. You have to get free in Christ. But there is value in accountability.

Surround yourself with other guys that have integrity and purity. It will make things a lot easier than if you are the only guy around who wants to be pure. If you don't have any friends who want to maintain purity, then you don't have any friends. Pray for the right kind of people to be around you. Seek out the strong. Anyone can be a sleaze.

5. Set the standard

Most guys let the girl set the standard and then they can get away with whatever the girl allows. That isn't right. *You* set the standard and set it high. Then walk in the integrity and righteousness God has for you. She will highly respect it and you will be the hero.

Stand firm. Don't waver. Let God show you what is truly happening and you will be highly blessed!

6. Don't be alone with a woman

This is something that I have determined in my life and share it with everyone I can. I am *never* alone with a woman who isn't my wife. This makes things interesting most of the time. If a woman shows up for a session and there is no other woman available for a witness, she goes home without a session. As a man in ministry, this is extremely important. I make sure all the women around me know the rules.

As a young man or even an old guy, this is something the enemy can use to take us down. All it takes is an accusation or even a hint of something inappropriate to destroy a ministry.

When men allow themselves to be alone with a woman, they set themselves up for disaster. First the thoughts come, and then small acting out. Eventually it comes around to doing something you wish you hadn't. If you are never alone, the chances of staying clean are much better.

Principles for the Women

1. Find protection

If you have a Christian Father, talk to him about being your protection in the relationships you have. It should never be you that has to say no to a man. If you are not married, you shouldn't be training yourself to say no. You should always be preparing to say yes. If you have no protection other than yourself, you have a tough road ahead of yourself.

I firmly suggest that you surround yourself with people of integrity and that you don't date. Dating puts you under the influence of a man who may or may not be trying to keep you pure. Dating is divorce practice. You are learning how to try something and if you don't like it then get out and try another one until you like it. That is a bad premise to build a relationship. Can you trust the Lord enough for Him to find the right one for you?

This is how my children have operated and it is a very wonderful experience. They don't have the pressure of finding their own mate. They are letting the Lord do that for them and it has worked out amazingly well.

Even those who don't have a Christian Father can find a solid, mature, Christian that will function in that capacity. Your protection is important and it really is a blessing to know it is there.

2. Don't advertise

It is very hard to get women to understand that they are continually advertising their sexuality. Most of that is men's fault. We have made you compete for attention and compare yourselves with each other. We have complimented you on sexy outfits and have shown you how much we approve of you showing off your body. Now it is true in our society that if you aren't looking sexy, you aren't looking good. Everything is supposed to be sexy.

The belief has come to women that if they aren't sexy enough, they won't go very far. That is quite true in most work places. It doesn't have to be true in the body of Christ. It shouldn't be true in gaining relationships. Being sexy isn't a good foundation to build a relationship on. If a man won't talk to you because you aren't sexy enough, then you don't want to talk to him anyway.

I will use this time to say something I want to say everywhere I go. Please, cover your body. I don't need to see your cleavage. I don't need to see your thighs. I don't need to see your midriff. When you put on an outfit, really look at it in the mirror. Bend over and see how much we see when you do that. Sit down and cross your legs and see how much we see when you are at Starbucks talking to your friends. You would be amazed at how really short shorts can be. You are just trying to look good and be comfortable. I understand. I hope you understand that there are men everywhere trying to see how much of your body they can see.

Young women are pleased when they see young guys look at them and approve. They are just trying to be accepted and get some attention from these hot guys they know. It isn't just the young guys that are attracted. It is also the skanky, old perverts out there that are getting a real thrill out of what you are (or are not) wearing. Just keep that in mind.

3. Men aren't women

Men don't think the same way women do. We recognize that in most areas, but not always when it comes to sex. To a female, a kiss is a sharing of friendship and just being close. To a guy, a kiss is getting the engine running for sex. Every kiss is sexual to the male mind. What you give is more than what you think you are giving. Women are always saying that men are animals. It is truer than you know. If he doesn't have any integrity, he is just trying to get what he can. Be wise. Be safe. Don't play with fire.

4. Fantasy

Men have fantasies, that is well known. The whole pornography industry is there because of men's fantasies. Women are just as bad, but no one seems to know it. Romantic novels, soap operas, and things like these are the pornography that women use. Women fantasize. About a man who will come and sweep them off their feet and actually take care of them and give them security.

Just like men's fantasies are bad, so are women's. All fantasies are just lies that we are allowing our minds to play with. When a man comes along and acts like a woman's fantasy man and treats her nicely, the thoughts then start and the enemy is opening up a door that is very dangerous.

Just like no woman can match a man's fantasy woman, no man can match a woman's fantasy man.

The man you are married to will never live up to that fantasy man. After a while, nothing he does is good enough and you will be looking for your right man to show up. Beware! It is a set up from the enemy. You need to lay down your soul for your husband and let God show you how He sees him and help him become the man God called him to be.

5. Never be alone with a man

The same principles rule here. If you are never alone, you will find it much easier to behave correctly. You will also not be putting yourself in the place of having to protect yourself. Being alone with a man puts pressure on the whole situation. You can cause him to have thoughts he wouldn't have had normally. If you become a target, you will be shot at with his thoughts.

Final thoughts

Again, I am only stating some principles. In our relationships, we must be careful and full of integrity. We need to treat the opposite sex the way Jesus would have us treat them. Always love and never lust. We don't have to fall the way so many have fallen. We need to have our ministries grow and develop the way God would have them be. Sexual impropriety will ruin things and take us out of the ministry and cause real damage.

Be wise.

CHAPTER NINE

FRIENDSHIPS

"I want to be your friend."

This request was delivered to me by one of the guys I had been spending quite a bit of time with out of my congregation. I had known him for a few years. He was born again under my ministry and had been growing consistently in his faith walk. He had become a constant presence every time the church doors were opened and we had fellowship times rather regularly. His boy played with my kids nearly every day. By any outside standard, he was my friend.

Why then was this such a deep request? Because I had taught him the different levels of friendship and he felt he understood what he was asking.

Being my friend meant that by being around us, spiritual warfare in his life would increase. He would need to be willing to go there. I thought about it for a while and even asked him if he understood what that entailed. He said he did. I then allowed him to come into my circle a little closer. I allowed him to see what I had to deal with during my encounters with people and the problems they faced. He experienced what I considered normal life for a pastor. He started interceding for me and watching for when I was tired and when I needed to back away for a season.

About six months later he came to me and during a normal conversation stated, "Being your friend ain't no picnic!"

Even though I laughed at that, it has stuck with me. It is true. Friendship with me means being exposed to the things I do all the time. It means walking in places that are not normally thought of as places to go. Most congregations do not understand the levels of damage available for people who walk in ministry. They just don't understand the depth of pain and heartache we open ourselves up to and how we just think of it as normal.

Why do we guard ourselves? Why is it so difficult for people in ministry to have close friends? The job of friend is deeper than most realize and the damage that can come from a friend is usually more than most ministers are willing to open themselves up to. That is why this chapter is so important.

But even if you don't consider yourself a minister, your friendships can make or destroy your life. These people are the most important and influential people in your life. Examining the realm of friendship is crucial to the health of each one of us.

I am consistently talking to people who have made amazingly bad decisions based solely on what a friend told them. Advice from a friend seems to hold more weight than advice from an expert. We tend to not trust experts, but we will trust a friend who has no idea what they are talking about. What does the Bible have to say about friendship? Anything important? I think so.

Let's examine a few of the stories in the Bible first and then some principles involved.

David and Jonathan

They were an unlikely pair. David had nothing. There is evidence that he was possibly illegitimate. After he killed Goliath, he was given the position of living in the King's house as a hero. After Saul saw that the people favored David more than they did him, he started to become jealous and hated David. Saul's son, however, found something in David that he had never seen before. Jonathan had everything, being the king's son, and he wanted to do something for David. He and David had such a deep friendship that is hard to comprehend.

Jonathan cut a covenant with David. It was a covenant of a stronger one (Jonathan) taking care of a weaker one (David). David received tokens from Jonathan to care for David in a new identity, in provision, and in protection. 1 Samuel 18:1 gives us information of great importance. It says the soul of Jonathan was knit to the soul of David and that he loved David as his own soul.

We talked about this in the chapter on soul ties. This is a good soul tie. It is the depth of emotion that is so significant here; it is a high level of commitment to one another and caring for one another. They are constant companions and they look out for each other for the rest of their lives.

Saul started looking for a way to kill David. David was street smart enough to recognize the signs and run. Jonathan wasn't so easily convinced that his father would do such a thing, however, Jonathan became a spy in his own household for David to find out how safe it was. David and Jonathan worked up a way of communicating how great the danger was and Jonathan found out it was real. David didn't want to do anything to put Jonathan in trouble at home and Jonathan was willing to give it all up for the sake of David. Such was the depth of their commitment to each other.

It is recorded in 1 Samuel 20:17 that Jonathan loved David as his own soul. This is as close as it gets to laying down one's soul in the Old Testament. As you discovered in Chapter 3, there is no greater love than to lay down your soul for your friend. The advantage we have under the New Covenant is that we have a very personal relationship with the Father. We aren't just laying down our selfishness for someone which can be done in the flesh, but we are actually laying down our soul to the Father and taking up His soul for someone. It is a highly spiritual function that overpowers our soulish functions in ways they couldn't understand in the Old Covenant. The indwelling of the Holy Spirit makes what we have in Christ exponentially higher and incredibly more personal.

What Jonathan and David had was the best example of love in the Old Testament. There was no selfishness in it. They truly lived for the other. Outstanding!

2 Samuel 1:26 makes a statement that proves my point in such a strong way. After the death of Saul and Jonathan, David wrote a lament for them. He refused to hate Saul but continually referred to him as the anointed of Jehovah. But to Jonathan he wrote, "I am distressed over you, my brother Jonathan. You were very delightful to me; your love was wonderful to me, more than the love of women." He was a true covenant blood brother to Jonathan. David had seen the love of women in Michal, Saul's daughter, who despised him and was taken away and given to another, and wasn't all that impressed by it. He married Abigail, the wife of Nabal, and that seemed good, but we don't know what happened to her. He had six wives (including Abigail and not counting Michal) while he was reigning in Hebron and then Jerusalem. Then he took Bathsheba in an adulterous affair making seven. He didn't have a good perspective about the love of women. He did, however, have a wonderful view of an incredibly powerful friendship with Jonathan and he valued it above all the relationships he had with women.

I've heard people try to pervert the meaning here and promote that David and Jonathan had a homosexual relationship. Absolutely absurd! David was writing a large selection of the Psalms at this time and everything was about being close to the heart of God. Perverting this to drag it down to something so menial and demeaning is pathetic and horrible. When I hear people say that, I have extreme pity for them because it is obvious that they can't see anything deeper than sexual sensuality for the basis of emotion. That is too bad. Such a tragedy to lessen friendship to sex. Real friends wouldn't do that and those who have, regret it with a deep remorse. As I write about friendship and know that I have to address this issue, it causes great sadness in my heart. To talk about the great beauty and then defile it with this discussion is disgusting, but it had to be pointed out.

David thought so much of Jonathan that he even sought out ways to bless his family after Jonathan died. One of the most beautiful stories is about how David blesses a crippled son of Jonathan, Mephibosheth. David gave him the same benefits that Jonathan gave David when he was first coming to Saul's house: robe, provision, a house, servants, a place at David's table, everything he needed and could want to live. David's desire was to honor Jonathan in every way possible, even after his death. That is true friendship.

David and Hushai

In 2 Samuel 15, David is dealing with the insurrection lead by Absalom. He is running from the city and is met by his friend Hushai. David tells him that if he goes with David, then it will be a burden on him, presumably because everyone going with him was in danger of being killed by Absalom. Instead, David knew he could trust Hushai because they were close friends. They obviously had dealings with each other before. David knew of certain traits that Hushai had that others didn't necessarily know. David sent Hushai to be a spy and a bad counsel to Absalom. David asked Hushai to risk his life for him. Hushai did it quickly without even considering the cost. What a friend.

Absalom knew his father's friends. When he saw Hushai, it caught him as odd and he even asked him, "What are you doing here, since you are a friend to my father?" It was unheard of for a friend to betray someone like David since he had such deep relationships with the men he chose as friends. It was so remarkable that Absalom almost didn't buy it. Hushai appealed to the vanity of Absalom by telling him that he followed those who sat on the throne and this was fitting to serve Absalom as he served his father. Absalom received him in his counsel. That was exactly why David sent him.

David's military advisor was Ahithophel. He was a brilliant strategist and understood the ways of gaining position over someone in power. Everything he told Absalom was very good advice. In fact, the Bible tells us that everything Ahithophel said was as if he heard it from Jehovah. That is one highly valuable advisor! David sent Hushai to mess with Ahithophel's counsel. David had other spies in the sons of the priests. Together they had a conspiracy that was their only weapon against Absalom and Ahithophel.

Ahithophel told Absalom what to do and it would have been the ruin of David if he had done it. But instead he wanted to hear what Hushai said. Hushai knew that Absalom wasn't the fearless person David was and used David's reputation as a mighty man of valor to scare Absalom into not acting quickly and it gave David time to get away to a place of safety. It saved David's life. When Ahithophel saw that Hushai's counsel was used instead of his, he went home and killed himself. He saw what was going to happen and knew that he would be counted as a traitor when David returned. This all turned out to be the downfall of Absalom and the return of David to the throne. Friends can be a powerful weapon.

David and Uriah

David had reigned for some time and decided not to go out to war with his troops. He stayed home in comfort and rest. One day he went up on the roof and happened to see a woman taking a bath on her rooftop. He lusted after her and sent for information about her. He wanted to know if she was available for him to have relations with her. He found out she was Bethsheba, the wife of Uriah the Hittite. That is remarkable because of something we will discover later. What was bad was that it didn't slow him down any. He called for her and had sex with her. It doesn't really matter if she was consenting, he was the king and she was to do as she was told. In essence, he raped her using his authority.

After a period of time, she discovered she was pregnant. David's sin had produced evidence that wasn't just going to go away. His shame (or the fear of it) prompted him to call Uriah home from the war with the purpose of him going home to his wife and then the pregnancy could be explained as his child. Uriah had too much integrity. He wouldn't go home. He didn't feel it was right to go to his house to spend the night in comfort when the army was out in the field. He didn't want to go to his wife because the troops couldn't go to their wives. David had a big problem.

David even tried to get Uriah drunk, but that didn't work either. He slept where the servants sleep and didn't go home. That really put David in a bind. His solution wasn't a good one.

David should have humbled himself and confessed, but he didn't. One sin led to another and now he was in the thick of it with very little recourse. He wrote a letter to Joab, the commander of the army and sent it back with Uriah. The letter told Joab to use the army to murder Uriah. It cost many men their lives and damaged the respect Joab had for David.

When word came that Uriah had died, David took Bathsheba as his wife. She had the baby in David's house. I'm sure many thought Uriah had gone home and that the baby was his. David didn't get away with anything, but most think that is the worst of the matter. There is much more to consider about this.

In 1 Kings 15:5, it tells us something very powerful. It is talking about how Abijam became king of Judah for a short period. Describing his reign, it also tells about how God is treating him because of his father David and the promises God made to him. It says in verse 5 that David was obedient to everything God told him to do all his life except in the matter of Uriah the Hittite.

What? It didn't say in the matter of Bathsheba or even in the matter of murder. It said in the matter of Uriah the Hittite. What made it so bad that David betrayed Uriah? Let's look at the evidence a bit closer.

In 2 Samuel 23:39, it lists David's mighty men. These are the men that came to David when he was on the run from Saul. They were outcasts and runaways from society, but they fit into David's needs very well. These guys stuck with David and did everything David asked of them in a very hard situation. They lasted for a long time. They were still with him when he won over Saul. They were still there when David was made king. These were David's closest friends who were there for him in all his worst times. Listed is Uriah the Hittite.

Uriah was a personal friend of David's. He was under the protective covenant of David to stick together and fight for each other while on the run. That covenant didn't run out. When David took Uriah's wife, he betrayed a covenant friend.

When David called Uriah home from the war to go in to his wife, he came straight to David and acted as if he really knew David because he really did. When David asked him why he didn't go home, it wasn't like a king telling him what to do, but as a friend that was talking to him. David even drank with him until he got Uriah drunk and that wasn't exceptional because he was one of his friends. Uriah trusted him so much that he was able to carry his own death sentence to Joab without any suspicion. Betrayal of a friend is very serious in God's eyes. It was the only thing God listed as what was between Him and David.

Job and His Friends

Volumes could be written about Job and the relationship with his friends. Job had real problems and his friends were there for him. They mourned for him from a distance as they first saw him and tore their robes. They came to him and just sat with him for seven days and seven nights without speaking anything. They did more than most of us would do for our friends. Job's suffering affected them deeply. They knew he was in pain both physically and in his soul for the loss of his family.

It is what came next that is so interesting. Job started talking. It primed the pump in his friends and pretty soon they started talking. All three of them said things to him that weren't right. Each of them was really trying to help. They were trying to find out why this was happening to Job. They thought if they could just find the sin that Job had done and get him to repent, then the suffering would be over. They misread the situation.

Their theology was incorrect and it made them think of God in the wrong light. Job had a good relationship with the Lord and was suffering for reasons he couldn't understand. He tried to defend himself and was doing quite well. His theology wasn't too bad.

Pretty soon, though, they got him talking the wrong way. A young man that was with them but wasn't listed as a friend of Job's spoke up and actually straitened them all out. After Elihu finished speaking, God spoke. He spoke directly to Job and not to his friends. That corrected Job's faulty thinking.

The Lord had things to say to Job's friends. God told them that they had spoken wrongly about Him, not correctly as Job had done. God told them that they had to bring sacrifices to Job and sacrifice repentance in front of him. They weren't to be forgiven until Job

171

prayed for them. That convinced them that Job was spiritually pure and not a sinner like they had thought and accused.

The most fascinating part is that when Job prayed for his three friends, his captivity was turned around. Everything was healed when he prayed healing and repentance for his friends. Maybe there is a great lesson for us there. Job was the one suffering, but it was his prayers for others that brought his freedom.

In this story, we have insight into friendship that needs to be learned. Even though there were mistakes made, everyone stuck it out with the others. Nothing seemed to be able to separate them. They visited each other when there was trouble, they sat with each other and didn't leave. Even after all the trouble, all of Job's friends gave him money. With that he rebuilt and God's blessings on him brought him much more than he had before all the trouble happened. His friends were still with him and they had knowledge of God between them that was the glue of their culture in relationship with each other. That is an amazing thing to learn from the book of Job.

Principles of Friendship

What does scripture say about friendship and the principles involved? It is one of the greatest relationships given to us. We have taken it quite lightly.

Exodus 33:10-11

And all the people would see the pillar of the cloud standing at the door of the tabernacle. And all the people rose and bowed themselves, each one at the door of his tent. And Jehovah would speak to Moses face to face, as a man speaks to his friend And he would return to the camp. And his attendant, Joshua the son of Nun, a young man did not leave the middle of the tabernacle.

What an amazing thing to say about a person, that Jehovah Himself would talk to you as a man talks to his friend. They didn't just talk business. It wasn't just worship. They talked. They talked about everything there was to be talked about. It was two entities coming together and discussing life and their feelings about it.

This is the goal of our Christian walk. We need to have that kind of relationship with our Lord, where we talk to Him as a man talks to his friend.

Moses had a unique relationship with the Lord. It wasn't offered to everyone around him, just Moses. Joshua didn't have one like it. Aaron, the High Priest, didn't have one like it. Only Moses. What did that look like? It was totally unique and we were given no more information about it.

Then the New Covenant comes and we are given the Holy Spirit to live inside us. We have a communion with God that Moses didn't have or know could be. With the indwelling of the Holy Spirit, we have access to the Father in close relationship like nothing known before except maybe by Adam before the fall. Yet we complain that we can't hear from God and that He is a million miles away. I think we have a problem and don't understand what we have. It is deeper than we know or experience. I think it is something we should pursue for the rest of our earthly days.

James 2:23

And the Scripture was fulfilled, saying, "And Abraham believed God, and it was counted for righteousness to him" and he was called, Friend of God.

Abraham also had a unique relationship with God. Since this is 400 years before the law, his relationship with the Father was one of covenant, not religion. God saw him as His friend. God takes this kind of relationship very seriously. He didn't roast Sodom without first talking to His covenant friend about it.

Abraham had enough confidence in that relationship to be able to actually negotiate with the Almighty about how many righteous there were in Sodom.

The key to it all is, however, that he believed God and that belief was counted to him for righteousness. His faith was the basis of the friendship with God Himself.

We have that relationship. Everything in our relationship with God is about faith and us trusting Him. If we spent more time getting to know Him and how to relate to Him, we would find that friendship with Him is the greatest thing in our lives.

Psalms 15:1-3

O Jehovah, who shall dwell in Your tabernacle? Who shall live in Your holy mountain? He who walks uprightly and works righteousness, and speaks the truth in his heart. He does not backbite with his tongue, nor does evil to his friend, nor lifts up a reproach against his neighbor.

Listed as one of the ways a person knows if he is walking uprightly in righteousness is that he doesn't do evil to his friend. Friendship is regarded as a very high thing that shouldn't be messed with. Friendship should be taken seriously and not reproached. Too often we hear about someone who betrays a friend. This is something very important to the Lord. He considered Judas Iscariot as a friend. That betrayal is one of the deepest hurts known to man throughout history. Jesus even called him friend when he approached Him in the garden. Friendship is important.

Proverbs 17:17

A friend loves at every time, but a brother is born for distress.

A true friend isn't one who only loves at a certain time. A true friend loves all the time, no matter what. Knowing that, it makes what the Lord told His disciples even more profound when He called them friends and no longer slaves. When they all left Him and abandoned Him at His crucifixion, it left Him completely alone to bear the sin. Even though they forsook Him, He didn't forsake them. He came back to them and gave them everything He had purchased on the cross.

Proverbs 18:24

A man of friends may be broken up, but there is a Lover who sticks closer than a brother.

This continues the thought as we know that Jesus is a lover that sticks closer than any friend or brother. That should make us really pursue the kind of friendship He emulates.

Proverbs 27:9

Ointment and perfume rejoice the heart, and one's friend is sweet from the counsel of the soul.

As one who has been through several tough situations, I know how sweet the counsel is of a friend who sticks with you. I have a few real friends that I know will be there for me no matter what happens. Just having that knowledge is a huge comfort for me and is very sweet to my soul. I can open myself up to them and they will not condemn me even though they may tell me I am in the wrong. Knowing they will give me the kind of counsel that will bring me closer to the Lord and be wise is of great value to me. I pray all will have those kinds of true friends.

Proverbs 27:10

Do not forsake your friend, nor your father's friend, and do not go into your brother's house in the day of your calamity, for a near neighbor is better than a brother far away.

Being there for others is as important as friends being there for you. I want to be the kind of friend that others can come to in their calamity. No matter how far away their family is, I want them to be able to come to me to find help. Even the friendships my father had should be valued by me and respected. I must be able to be trusted for them. The best thing I can do is to be the constant witness for the things of the Lord.

Everyone should know that I will act in accordance to the scripture in every situation. They should be able to count on that. That is the best kind of love and friendship I could have for them. The best thing I can do is to be the representative of the Lord to them and consistently take people to Him, no matter what they have done or what has happened to them. My consistency is what will be of value to them now and no matter how long from now.

Proverbs 27:17

Iron sharpens iron, so a man sharpens his friends face.

The biggest problem with this verse is that iron doesn't sharpen iron. One of my hobbies is working with iron on a forge. If I take two pieces of iron and rub them together, it will take forever to get either of them sharp. If two people are totally equal in their existence, they have nothing to help the other one out with. What sharpens iron is harder iron.

When iron has been through the fire and beaten into shape and heated and quenched in the proper way, it becomes hardened. A file is hardened iron. It can be used to sharpen iron. In this way, the analogy really works.

If a man has been through the fire and beaten into shape, he knows that the Lord is good for it in those situations. He becomes valuable like a file is valuable and able to be used. He then is able to help his friend to become a better person, because he himself has been through it.

The face of a man is his identity. If I am sharpening my friends face, I am taking things off him that shouldn't be there for him to have the kind of identity he needs to have in this life. As I disciple people, I am constantly filing away things in their lives that shouldn't be there and helping them see who they really are in Christ Jesus. I am sharpening their faces. If I hadn't gone through the things I have gone through, I wouldn't have the experience of seeing Jesus work and I also wouldn't have the resources I have for helping people. I have been pounded into something the Master can use to sharpen people's identities in Him.

I really appreciate meeting people and getting to know the things they have been through. I realize they have a lot to offer and if I am wise, I will listen and let them sharpen my face so I can be better and better for the Master to use. As it says in Proverbs 13:20, "He who walks with the wise shall be wise." That is what I want.

Proverbs 22:24-25

Do not feed a possessor of anger, and do not go in with a man of fury, lest you learn his ways and take a snare for your soul.

The scripture does have warnings about having the wrong kind of friends. Friends have a way of getting us to do things we wouldn't normally do. That can be good as we influence our friends to walk with Jesus, or it can be bad as we influence each other to walk outside the wisdom of God.

Hanging out with folks who are angry will just make us angry. As we listen to people who are disgruntled or hurt in some way, we tend to take their side and get mad with them. That is taking up an offence. As we found out earlier, that is extremely dangerous.

I will hang out with an angry person just long enough for them to either get rid of their anger or reject me as a friend. I will not idly stand by and let him self-destruct. I will give him wise counsel and offer to minister to him in his time of trouble, but it usually doesn't take long for him to get mad at me and tell me to go away. After he has calmed down, he may come to me and receive ministry or get counsel in how to make up for the dumb things he did while he was angry. If not, he will find something in me that offends him and walk away from me. Either way he will know that I will respond in a certain way and will do so consistently over many years.

I have heard it said that either you are a thermostat or a thermometer. A thermometer just goes up and down with the temperature of what is happening around them. A thermostat actually brings changes to the area and is a tool to get things where it needs to be. I want to be the person that affects my surroundings, not just respond to them. This makes things a little difficult in people's lives, but I refuse to be affected by their poor choices. The outcome is that after many years of being like this, I have several stories of people who have eventually come around to the things of the Lord and have told me that they are very glad I was there for them and that I didn't change. It was quite a comfort for them that I was still there for them no matter what they have done or how deeply they have gotten into trouble. I choose to be a thermostat.

1 Corinthians 15:33

Do not be led astray; bad companionships ruin good habits.

Right out of the New Covenant, we are warned again. Just because we are believers in Jesus Christ, doesn't mean that there aren't bad companions out there. We are constantly barraged with bad counsel and people who don't know what they are talking about. We must be careful.

As my children were growing up, it was a common form of irritation to me to see the kind of kids my kids brought home. Since I couldn't be around them all the time and chase away the kids that I didn't want hanging around my kids, I had to come up with another strategy. I taught my kids to influence them!

I had to show them how to respond in just about every kind of situation imaginable. I would watch them and when we were alone I would coach them on what I saw. I taught them to love everyone, but to not be influenced by how the other people acted or thought. What I came up with is all three of my children grew up to be leaders and not followers. I will take that any day of the week!

I have watched as all of my children have had real loser friends, but have taken them to the Father in many different ways. Not all their friends have accepted the ministry that was offered to them, and some have fallen away terribly, but my kids have always been there for their friends over many years and have been consistently walking the Christian walk in front of all their friends. They are equipped and I couldn't be more proud of them. They are good friends.

Jesus

It wouldn't be complete to talk about friendships without talking about Jesus. He knew what a real friendship was. He understood the deep relationship that was truly beneficial in having a friend and how to treat one. He had many who followed Him, but he only had a few that were really close to Him.

He treated Peter, James, and John differently. He took them with Him up on the Mount of Transfiguration and allowed them to witness His discussion with Elijah and Moses. He didn't even let them tell it to anyone else. It made an impact on them.

They even knew how to use it to their advantage. At the last Passover meal, John even leaned over on Jesus and asked Him who it was that was going to betray Him. John always called himself the one that Jesus loved. Peter knew the depth of his denial and how personal it was. He needed restoration that happened when Jesus asked him if he loved Him.

In His time of deepest trouble, in Gethsemane, He asked those three to come be with Him as He poured out His soul to the Father. They didn't always respond correctly, nor did they live up to what they should have done. That didn't detract from their relationship with Jesus, He just took it in stride and loved them. Even after the resurrection, Jesus had James and John tell Peter specifically that He had risen from the dead.

Of all the scripture passages referenced in this book, one stands out as the foundation for everything else. Even in that passage, there is more to be said.

John 15:13

Greater love than this has no one, that anyone should lay down his soul for his friends.

Laying down our souls is how we love someone, or anyone. That is how we get greater love. But the verse actually says 'for his friends'.

Laying down our souls is how we love someone or anyone. That is how we get greater love. But the verse actually says "for his friends."

It starts with our friends. It is easier to learn to lay down your soul with someone you already like and have a relationship with. Friends don't usually have a lot of junk between them to deal with. They always have some, but it isn't enough to break them apart permanently. We don't usually live with friends, but we have occasion to seek their presence and we want to be with them. This is a good basis for learning to love.

Jesus started it with telling us in John 10 that He is the Good Shepherd and that He laid down His soul for the sheep. He considered His friends to be those the Father gave Him to care for and to bring abundant life. So, He gives us a mandate to follow:

1 John 3:16

By this we have known the love of God, because that One laid down His soul for us; and on behalf of the brothers we ought to lay down our souls.

"Greater love" is laying down your soul for your friends. Jesus laid down His soul for the sheep. That makes the sheep His friends.

We are to lay down our souls for the brothers. That makes the brothers our friends. We are to have relationships in the body of Christ that are deep and intimate. We are to be laying down what we feel for them and picking up what the Father feels. We are to be laying down what we think of them and picking up what the Father thinks of them. We are to be laying down what we want for them (or what we want for ourselves from them) and pick up what the Father wants for them (and, in the meantime, getting our needs met in the Father, not through friends).

When we do this, we become the best friends anyone could possibly want. We will do whatever is necessary to help our friends and not hurt them. That means we won't help them sin. On the contrary, we will help them get out of their junk and into living the way the Lord would have them live. A good friend is one who will fight for you and get you free to live a life of freedom in Jesus Christ. A good friend will tell you the truth and not pacify you with what you want to hear.

I hear people all the time telling me that a friend of theirs wanted them to go with them into some form of sinful stupidity. I tell them that that person isn't their friend. A real friend wouldn't get you into that kind of trouble. A real friend would get you out of it, not into it. A real friend is a godly friend. I am a good friend if I am helping someone become all that God would have them be. If I see them the way the Lord sees them, I won't be fulfilled as a friend until they see themselves that way and are helped to become it. That is an awesome friend.

Jesus told us more about what being a friend is all about. Look at these verses:

John 15:13-15

Greater love than this has no one, that anyone should lay down his soul for his friends. You are My friends if you do whatever I command you. I no longer call you slaves, for the slave does not know what his lord does. But I called you friends, because all things which I heard from My Father I made known to you.

A true friend is one who links his life up with his friend for a common purpose. A true friend of Jesus is one who is aligned with what Jesus is doing on the earth. It isn't about what I get out of it, but what I am willing to do for Him and the cause that He has. It isn't about blindly being a slave and doing something I am told, but being a part of something. I am doing what I am told to do for the reason that it advances my friend Jesus. I am not a robot, but a willing participant in the greater scheme of things on this planet. I am one with Him and with the Father. To do my part, I have to be submitted and obedient. I have to have a relationship with Him in everything I am doing and everything He wants me to be a part of.

This John 15 passage goes on to talk about how we treat each other in love and how we are part of the greater whole with each other. We are all in this together. We actually need each other. We better start laying down our souls for each other and learn how to live together in common purpose instead of rejecting everyone and doing our own thing.

Vulnerability is always a part of being a friend. A friend is able to hurt someone more than an enemy. Being vulnerable is trusting someone else with our safety and well-being. We can talk to them, share things with them that we wouldn't share with others, and we trust that we will continue to be safe. When a friend betrays us, it is a deeper hurt than almost anyone can do to us. When people who we think are friends betray us, it is much more difficult to be able to trust someone else.

Jesus knew this better than anyone. Everyone abandoned Him and fled. He was totally alone on the cross and His Father even turned His back on Him. He was the only one who could carry our sin and He bore it completely alone. We think that Peter, James, and John should have stuck up for Him, but it wasn't them who He felt badly for. It was Judas.

Judas was with Jesus for three years and was trusted enough to carry the money for the team. He also went out with another disciple as they were sent to go and heal the sick, raise the dead, cast out demons, and preach the gospel of the kingdom. He was also there when Jesus washed their feet at the last Passover. He started the Passover with Him and then left after the first sop, the dipping of the unleavened bread into the bitter herbs. He left in bitterness and didn't partake of the redemption that was promised in the rest of the meal. Everyone was faked out but Jesus. They all thought he was going out to do a good deed. They didn't see him for what he truly was, one who choose perdition instead of the salvation that was offered to him. How did this affect Jesus? I'm sure He had this running through His head:

Psalm 55:12-14

For it is not an enemy reproaching me, or I could bear it; it is not one who hates me who is magnifying himself against me; or I would hide myself from him. But it is you, a man of my rank, my friend and my associate. We sweetened counsel together; we marched into the house of God with the throng.

It wasn't a bad guy; it was His friend who betrayed Him. How deep was this betrayal? Look at what happened:

Matthew 26:47-50

And as He was yet speaking, behold, Judas came, one of the Twelve. And with him was a numerous crowd with swords and clubs, from the chief priests and elders of the people. And the one betraying Him gave them a sign, saying, Whomever I may kiss, it is He; seize Him. And coming up at once to Jesus, he said, Hail, Rabbi. And he ardently kissed Him. But Jesus said to him, Friend, why are you here? Then coming up, they laid hands on Jesus and seized Him.

Jesus knew why Judas had come. He even made sure Judas had a way out, a path to repent. He even called Judas "friend" and in Luke it reports that Jesus asked him if he were betraying Him with a kiss, an obvious sign of affection and relationship. He knew He would lose this one, but it didn't make things any easier.

Psalm 41:9

Even a man desiring my welfare, I trusted in him, eating of my bread; this one has lifted up his heel against me.

Jesus knew the hurt of betrayal from a friend, and He still expects us to be vulnerable and open to people. He knows we will be hurt and that we can come to Him for the healing of that hurt. He wants us to be able to open ourselves up again for another to hurt us. We will then be loving as He is. He is continually open for relationship with people, knowing that He will be betrayed again and again. He wants us to be the same way, open to people and letting ourselves be vulnerable for them to hurt us. He wants us to know that we have a friend who sticks closer than a brother (Psalm 18:24) and that we can go to Him all the time.

In this manner, He shows Himself to be a constant friend to us, someone who will always be there and will walk with us in any part of life. I can be a friend because I have one that is constant and true. I can show Him to others and I know He is always there and working. What a deal!

It is a beautiful thing to understand friendships. It is just as beautiful to understand the relationship we have with Him and how He is empowering us to be friends with people and to show Him to them.

The Warning

Even at that, we must be careful with our friendships. They can only be good if they are in Him. The rest will be damaging to our lives.

James 4:4-5

Adulterers and adulteresses! Do you not know that the friendship of the world is enmity with God? Whoever, then, purposes to be a friend of the world is put down as hostile to God. Or do you think that vainly the Scripture says, The spirit which has dwelt in us yearns to envy?

God is a jealous God. His name is Jealous (Exodus 34:14). He wants us only for Himself. Everything else is idolatry and adultery.

The friendship that Jesus talked about is a covenant friend, one who dies to Himself and lives for the other person for the rest of his life. He did that for us and He expects no less from us. A total commitment gives back total benefit.

1 John 2:15

Do not love the world nor the things in the world. If anyone loves the world, the love of the Father is not in him

May we be the friends of God the Father, Son, and Holy Spirit.

CHAPTER TEN

SPIRITUAL AUTHORITY

Teaching the principles of spiritual authority shows us how to treat those who are in authority over us and under us. This understanding can save a lot of people a lot of pain and damage. Few subjects have been so misunderstood.

In all my years of ministry (at this writing it is close to forty-five years), I have very seldom seen churches understand what spiritual authority is. I've seen it abused (causing severe damage in many believers) and I've seen it neglected (causing severe damage in many believers). The Lord has a much better way of dealing with things. When we understand how it works, we are much better able to handle what needs to be done and how to actually get things accomplished for the Kingdom.

The problem is that people associate position for value. We think that if someone is above us in authority, they are better than we are. That is far from the truth. That simple lie has caused many of the problems facing the church today. People fight being under someone else because they feel it makes them a lesser person and they are fighting for validity and value. God doesn't see people that way. Value isn't determined by position; you don't need to climb the ladder to get higher in God's eyes. In fact, it is just the opposite.

Jesus had to deal with this among His disciples. They were continually jockeying for position and trying to see which of them would be greater in the Kingdom. Jesus had to talk to them about it in several passages.

They were comparing themselves and what they had done in ministry which will never turn out well.

Mark 9:33-35

And they came to Capernaum. And having come into the house, He questioned them, What were you disputing to yourselves in the way? And they were silent, for they argued with one another in the way as to who was greater. And sitting, He called the Twelve and said to them, If anyone desires to be first, he shall be last of all and servant of all.

Jesus' structure was upside down to them. The one who serves is the greatest, not the one who leads. The reason for that is amazing. The one who dies to himself the most is the one who can serve best. The one who is dead to himself is the one who can let the Lord live through him. The greatest is the one who lets Jesus live through him the most.

Matthew 20:20-28

Then the mother of the sons of Zebedee came near to Him, along with her sons, worshipping, and asking something from Him. And He said to her, What do you desire? She said to Him, Say that these two sons of mine may sit one on Your right, and one on Your left in Your Kingdom. But answering, Jesus said, You do not know what you ask. Are you able to drink the cup which I am about to drink, and to be baptized with the baptism with which I am to be baptized? They said to Him, We are able. And He said to them, Indeed you shall drink My cup, and you shall be baptized with the baptism with which I am baptized; but to sit off My right and off My left hand is not Mine to give, but to those for whom it was prepared by My Father. And hearing, the ten were indignant about the two brothers. But having called them, Jesus said, You know that the rulers of the nations exercise lordship over them, and the great ones exercise authority over them. But it will not be so among you. But whoever desires to become great among you, let him be your servant. And whoever desires to be first among you, let him be your servant; Even as the Son of Man did not come to be served, but to serve, and to give His life a ransom for many.

This passage offers great insight into God's kingdom authority. Jesus didn't rebuke her for asking. He just told her it wasn't His position to grant that request. He did address the issue, though. He asked them if they were able to drink the cup that He was going to drink and to be baptized with the same baptism. He was referring to the cup of Gethsemane, the cup of total submission to the will of the Father. He was referring to the baptism of fire of being martyred. They said they were able.

This was the issue exactly. To be in that kind of leadership, they had to be able to give up of themselves and their selfishness completely. They had to die to their own agendas so that they had only the agenda of the Father in their minds and focus. Jesus told them of the requirements and they thought they could do it. What is really interesting is that He said that they would! And they did! But they had to go through many things before they would be able to say that they had done it.

The other disciples were very angry when they heard about this. Jesus didn't tell them that James and John and their mother were wrong in asking for a high position. He had used it as an opportunity to personally teach them a very personal lesson. The other ten didn't like it very much.

Servanthood is frowned upon in the world. Serving others is a lesser task to humans, but to God it is a higher task. Jesus, who was the greatest leader ever, said that He didn't come to be served, but to serve and to give His soul as a ransom for many. He demonstrated His teaching of the laying down of the soul as the highest form of love. He said that until you do that and actually love people, you can't be trusted to lead them. The more you lay down your soul, the more you love, and the more you can lead without any personal agenda. We don't see it as all that important, but God does. It appears that submission is one of the highest ways of being Godly.

Submission isn't a dirty word. Every organization needs a system of authority to make it work. God puts us into the structure in the exact place that prepares us for greater growth. He puts us in places that will also be the best for those around us. Only He knows the full agenda. We are going to have to trust Him and yield to His will to be obedient. It just isn't easy all the time.

Scripture has been given to us to show us what the Lord thinks about this subject. He had the New Testament written in Greek so we can have understanding to a fine point. Let's look.

Romans 13:1-2

Let every soul be subject to higher authorities, for there is no authority except from God, but the existing authorities have been ordained by God. So that the one resisting authority has opposed the ordinance of God, and the ones opposing will receive judgment to themselves.

This starts with telling every soul that they need to do something. This means everyone who thinks, feels, and wants. He isn't talking to robots who have no will or feelings or thoughts about things. He is talking to people. Everyone who has a soul is commanded to be subject. It is our choice.

The Greek word for subject is the word *hupotasso*. It comes from two words: *hupo* meaning under, and *tasso* meaning order. It means to be under the order or structure. You have to place yourself under someone else to be under the order. God set up an order, and instructed you to submit to it. You should not strive to be at the top. There should always be someone you are submitted to.

It says that every soul has to be under the order of higher authorities. There is always someone to submit to or to pursue being submitted to. In times of war, stories are told about soldiers on patrol who have lost their commander. Someone has to assume command in order for there to be a leader. Without a leader, the team just falls into chaos and misdirection. The next in rank takes the position of authority and assumes command. The team must follow the new commands of the new commander. A wise commander takes in all the information he can and the counsel of those around him, then he must make decisions and give commands. Even though he is in command of this group of men, he is constantly trying to get them back to headquarters alive and with the mission fulfilled. He is working hard to get back to where he is under the authority of someone else. Even while in the field, he knows he is under orders about what they are doing and the mission they are under. Authority is highly important and each one needs to be submitted to it.

The issue is that you are not the highest authority. You need to be submitted. Why? Because there is no authority except from God Himself. It is basically all under Him and put in place for us to be able to do what He has called us to do. There have been many times in my life that I was under a bad boss or someone who was making my life as miserable as possible. I was still commanded to submit to them as if they were from God Himself, because they were! I had to learn how to think and how to act under someone who was incompetent but still in charge. It was very humbling (maybe that is why God put me under them!). There is always something God was trying to teach me and every time I humbled myself and submitted to their authority, I came out on top and highly benefited. Every lesson learned in that way equipped me to be able to do so much more for the Lord later on. One of the biggest lessons was to learn to submit.

It says in Romans 13 that every existing authority is ordained by God. The Greek word for ordained is *tetasso*. As we saw previously, *tasso* means order. The prefix *te* means to be placed. *Tetasso* means to be placed in order. The existing authorities have been placed in order by God Himself. I would be wise to submit to them, since I am actually submitting to God and not to man alone. Knowing that, I am much more prone to submit to them knowing God is to be trusted and He has my benefit in mind.

Verse 2 says that the person who resists that authority opposes the ordinance of God. The Greek word for resist is *antitasso*. *Anti* means against or opposite and *tasso* means order. *Antitasso* means against the order of. The Greek word for ordinance is *diatasso*. *Dia* means through, and *tasso* is the order. The ordinance of God is intended to bring us through to the other side of something and if we submit to it, we will be brought to the place where God wants us. If we resist it, we will be coming against the very order of God that He has for us.

The Greek word for the word opposed and opposing is *anthistemi*. It comes from two words, *anti*—against, and *histemi*—to stand. To stand against doesn't just mean to not do something, but to actively stand in a position of keeping it from happening, to actively try to stop it. If you aren't submitted to the authority, you are actually standing against God's plan to bring the things into your life that He wants to bring to you. It can't be good to stand against God.

In fact, this verse tells us that if we stand against Him and His plan, we will receive judgment to ourselves! When we negate God's plan of love, the only thing we have left is to stand before His justice. The much more intelligent thing to do then is to just submit to His working in our lives and trust Him to bring us through. When we don't submit, we are saying that we are in authority and that our authority is greater than God's. We are then standing opposing Him as an opposing god to fight with Him. It says that very thing in James and 1 Peter.

James 4:5-10

Or do you think that vainly the Scripture says, The spirit which has dwelt in us yearns to envy? But He gives greater grace. Because of this it says, "God sets Himself against proud ones, but He gives grace to humble ones." Then be subject to God. Resist the Devil, and he will flee from you. Draw near to God, and He will draw near to you. Cleanse your hands, sinners! And purify your hearts, double minded ones! Be distressed, and mourn, and weep. Let your laughter be turned to mourning, and your joy into shame. Be humbled before the Lord, and He will exalt you.

This states that God sets Himself against the proud one. "Sets against" is the Greek word *antitasso*. God is against the order of those who are proud. In our pride, we are setting up ourselves as the one who is in charge of all of it. We aren't and cannot be. But if we set ourselves in that place, God Himself will come against us.

"Be subject to God" is to be *hupotasso* to God or under His authority. This puts us in position to be able to *anthistemi* or stand against the devil. When we draw near to God in submission with a humble heart, being cleansed and walking His way, then He will exalt us and put us in the position He intends for us to have. 1 Peter makes this point even greater.

1 Peter 5:5-9

Likewise, younger ones be subject to older ones; and all being subject to one another. Put on humility, because God sets Himself "against proud ones, but He gives grace to humble ones." Then be humbled under the mighty hand of God, that He may exalt you in time; "casting all your anxiety onto Him," because it matters to Him concerning you. Be sensible, watch, because your adversary the Devil walks about as a roaring lion seeking someone he may devour; whom firmly resist in the faith, knowing the

same sufferings are being completed in your brother-
hood in the world.

Both of these passages tell us that we are in great need of humbling ourselves and submitting to the plan of God. We will then be
put in position to take on the enemy with great success. The enemy
has won so often in our lives because we weren't submitted to the
plan of God and were effectively living under the hand of the enemy
to do with as he wanted. We have no authority without submitting
to God.

But when we do submit to God and obey Him, we are put in
position of being under His hand and therefore under His protection. We then have His authority over the enemy and with His words
and direction are able to take the enemy out and bring the Kingdom
of God into function in our lives. We can relax, knowing that we are
in the camp of God and have His power and direction. We win!

Back to Romans 13. Now that we have seen that we are all to
be submitted to the authorities that God has ordained and not fighting Him, we see that there are some other things God wants us to
understand.

Romans 13:3-7

For the rulers are not a terror to good works, but to
the bad. And do you desire not to fear the authority?
Do the good, and you will have praise from it; for
it is a servant of God to you for the good. But if you
practice evil, be afraid; for it does not bear the sword
in vain; for it is a servant of God, an avenger for
wrath to the one practicing bad things. Because of
this, it is necessary to be subject, not only on account
of wrath, but also on account of conscience. For on
this account you also pay taxes, for they are ministers
of God, always giving attention to this very thing.
Then give to all their dues: to the one due tax, the

tax; to the one due tribute, the tribute; to the one
due fear, the fear; to the one due honor, the honor.

This tells us that every authority has some form of sword to use. There are always consequences for disobedience to those in authority over us. When we speed, the policeman has the ability to give us a ticket and get money from us. If we keep resisting, he has the ability to put is in jail. If we keep on resisting, he has a 9 millimeter sword at his disposal! The authorities in our lives are there as servants of God to bring us good. However, if we are bucking against the rule of those in authority over us, we are fighting what God is wanting to do in our lives.

We are told that it is necessary to be subject, not just to keep us out of wrath, but because of conscience. The reasons we are submitted are just as important as being submitted. We shouldn't be obedient to higher authorities just because we don't want them to give us a ticket or to not be afraid of them. We should be submitted because we want to be. Our attitude toward (or against) those above us is as important as our actual obedience.

If I am submitted to God first, and because of my relationship with Him, I will want to be submitted if for no other reason than because it blesses Him for me to do so. If I have a loving relationship with Him, then I can trust Him to work in my life in a way that will benefit me and bless Him. Not submitting to authorities is not trusting God, but thinking that I know more about what I need than He does. If I am trusting me instead of Him, then I am cursing the very situation I am in (Jeremiah 17:5-6). Not yielding to authority is about me being the god of my life and not letting God be who He is supposed to be.

Therefore, my attitude about things is very important. This passage goes on to tell us that we are to be paying taxes and giving to each what is due him. We are to do that lovingly and with a submitted heart. We are to do it because of our love for Him and not just because we are told to do it. We are to fear those whom we are supposed to fear and we are supposed to give honor to whomever we are supposed to give honor. It doesn't mean that they will always act in a manner that deserves it, but it is to be given anyway, because we are supposed to do so. We are commanded to honor our fathers and mothers. So many people I have met had fathers (or mothers) who weren't very good people. They were abusers, drunks, absent, molesters and many, many other things. Even though they weren't very good parents, we are still commanded to honor them. We must honor the position even though we may not appreciate the person who occupied that position.

I know a lot of people who are quite political in their views. They may not like the person who is in the office of president right now, but that doesn't give them any right to not honor the position. We are commanded to pray for those in authority over us so that we can have a peaceful life. It didn't say that we are only to pray for the ones we agree with. I have found that my attitude of honoring will help me have peace in the depth of some very bad situations. When I have an attitude of submission, I have a freedom that is hard to describe even though I am under an unreasonable authority. God is still watching out for us and taking care of us.

Hebrews 13:17

Yield to those taking the lead of you, and submit, for they watch for your souls, giving an account, that they may do this with joy, and not with grieving; for this would be unprofitable to you.

This is very interesting because it tells us that those in authority over us are actually watching for our souls. They will give an account to the Lord for what they do over us. They will stand before God for how they lead, I will stand before Him for how I followed and how I submitted. Leadership is in His hands, not mine.

It is my role to make their leadership something of beauty. I am to make them glad they have me under them. I must be a joy, not a pain.

I have experienced both ends of the spectrum on this principle and have seen how this works in my own life. I have been under good bosses and bad bosses.

When I submitted and let God work, His will worked in glorious ways. God's will is almost always accomplished in ways I didn't understand until much later. I have almost never understood what He was doing and why at the time. When I submitted anyway, I have seen God work out the worst problems and situations to bring about beautiful results. Even though I didn't understand what He was doing, if I submitted and did what I was supposed to do, I found peace in the situation and could trust Him to get me out of this situation. If I didn't submit and tried to manipulate things to get what I wanted, the turmoil inside me was devastating and I ended up bitter and still in trouble.

The same thing has been true for me as the one in leadership. I have had those who were submissive and worked to further the job and I have had those who fought me tooth and nail in every aspect of the job and made my life as the boss miserable.

In each situation, this passage proved itself to be very true. When my attitude was correct or when those under me had attitudes that were of God, we were able to accomplish just about anything. When my attitude or the attitude of those under me was bad, it was tough getting anything done and everyone suffered. Unfortunately, that is the very existence of so many in the work place today. Most of it is because of bad attitudes and not trusting the Lord to work.

The issue has been (and will continue to be) the condition of our souls. When our souls are healthy, we can have healthy outlooks on life and love. When our souls are damaged, we are responding out of our pain and need to defend and protect ourselves from that pain. We will continually be trusting ourselves for everything and the outcome is destructive. We need to have our souls and the issues in them healed so we can relax and trust in the Lord's loving hand. Then we can know that God will bring people into our lives to watch out for our souls. None of us is at the top of the heap. There is always someone over us who we are held accountable to. Even the CEO's of the largest companies will have to give an account of how they have treated those under them. Our Lord Jesus Christ will have them give an account as they stand before Him. That gives me great comfort.

This is why it says:

1 Peter 2:13-17

Then be in obedience to every creation of men because of the Lord; whether to a king, as being supreme; or to governors, as through Him having indeed being sent for vengeance on evildoers, but praise on well doers, because so is the will of God, doing good to silence the ignorance of foolish men; as free, and not having freedom as a cover of evil, but as slaves of God; honor all, love the brotherhood, fear God, honor the king.

We are to be submissive to all those above us in authority. That way we are showing people who watch us how to respond in life and how to live in God. We don't have our freedom in order to do whatever we want. We are first of all submitted to God and therefore able to yield to those in this world over us. Remember that Peter and Paul didn't have a good king over them. When Peter was written, the Emperor Nero was reigning and trying his hardest to blame Christians for burning Rome. Both Peter and Paul were martyred under him. That didn't matter, Peter still told us under the inspiration of the Holy Spirit to be in obedience to every authority and to honor the king. It is the will of God for us to be submissive and for the authority structure to lead wisely and take care of people. We don't have any control over whether an authority is submitted to God or not, but we do have the ability to choose to be submissive and trust God for the outcome.

The idea continues in this passage in Peter to tell the slaves to obey and submit even in bad situations. He says that it is better to submit and suffer for doing good than to rebel and suffer for doing evil. When we suffer for doing good, it is a grace of God. What is our attitude under unjust bosses? We should be holding them up before

God and letting Him deal with them. We are still told to be submissive. It isn't a suggestion; it is a command.

Jesus taught the same thing. He knew that those in authority weren't doing things correctly while He was teaching the disciples. He knew they were doing things for the wrong reasons and in the wrong way. He knew they didn't have a relationship with God, but He also knew they were in authority spiritually. He told the disciples and the Jews in Judea to submit. Look at what He told them:

Matthew 23:1-12

Then Jesus spoke to the crowd and to His disciples, saying, The scribes and the Pharisees have sat down on Moses' seat. Then all things, whatever they tell you to keep, keep and do. But do not do according to their works, for they say, and do not do. For they bind heavy and hard to bear burdens, and lay them on the shoulders of men, but they do not desire to move them with their finger. And they do all their works to be seen by men. And they make their phylacteries broad and enlarge the borders of their robes. And they love the first couch in the suppers, and the first seats in the synagogues, and the greetings in the markets, and to be called by men, Rabbi, Rabbi. But do not you be called Rabbi, for One is your Leader, the Christ, and you are all brothers. And call no one your father on earth, for One is your Father, the One in Heaven. Nor be called leaders, for One is your Leader, the Christ. But the greater of you shall be your servant. And whoever will exalt himself shall be humbled, and whoever will humble himself shall be exalted.

He said the Pharisees actually have authority, but they have misused it and needed to be confronted about it. Even though they were doing it wrong, He still said the people were to do what the Pharisees said. But the big thing was to not do what the Pharisees were doing. Their words were out of the scriptures, but their actions were out of themselves.

The heart of those in authority may not be right with God, but He does use them to work in our lives. We don't always see how that is going to work and we kick against the goads that God brings into our lives to help us. He can also use unbelievers in our lives to bring us what He wants us to have. We must be submitted to any authority over us, it doesn't matter their spiritual condition. God knows what we need and He uses every tool at His command to bring us into the position He knows is best for us. He knows we have things in our lives that are hindering our walk with Him. He uses spiritual authority to bring to us the understanding and exposure of what the hindrances are. That brings us closer to Him and helps us get rid of things in our lives that aren't supposed to be there. He will do some amazing things in our lives to show us what needs to be taken care of. Most of that will come from some form of spiritual authority in our lives. As we trust Him and know His way of working in us, we will discover how to grow in Him and become who we are supposed to be in Him.

The authorities in our lives will not always act correctly. How we respond to bad authority tells us more about ourselves than just about anything else. Can we stay submitted? Can we show humility or will we blow up in pride and destroy everything around us? It may be how we respond that brings that authority under the hand of God. They are watching our lives. We show them Jesus in the way we respond to them in all sorts of strange and wondrous situations. They put us in bad places to see us respond and to try to get us to fall. If we fall then they won't have to repent. They will use our bad responses as an excuse that they don't need God. They can ignore their need to come to Him.

2 Corinthians 10:8-18

For even if I also somewhat more fully should boast about our authority (which the Lord gave

*us for building up and not for your destruction),
I will not be put to shame; so that I may not seem
to frighten you by letters. Because, they say, the letters are weighty and strong, but the bodily presence
is weak, and his speech being despised. Let such a
one think this, that such as we are in word through
letters, being absent, such we are also being present
in deed. For we dare not rank or compare ourselves
with some of those commending themselves, but they
measuring themselves among themselves and comparing themselves to themselves, are not perceptive.
But we will not boast beyond measure, but according to measure of the rule which the God of measure
distributed to us, to reach even to you. For we do
not overstretch ourselves as if not reaching to you,
for we also came to you in the gospel of Christ, not
boasting beyond measure in the labors of others, but
having hope that the growing faith among you will
be made larger according to our rule, to overflow-
ing, in order to preach the gospel to that which is
beyond you, not to boast in another's rule in things
made ready. "But the one boasting, let him boast
in" the "Lord." For not the one commending himself
is the one approved, but the one whom the Lord
commends.*

Paul is boasting about his authority, but told us that it was to build up and not to tear down. He knew others would be compar-ing themselves to him and vice versa. He knew that such compari-sons would be fruitless. He also understood that his authority wasn't because of man's way of doing things. He wasn't showing himself as better than anyone because of the way he looked or his ability to speak. He didn't have to prove his authority by acting a certain way. He had the authority because God gave it to him.

But one of the greatest revelations in this passage is that he knew he didn't have total authority everywhere. He knew his authority only went to the Corinthians. He didn't want to overstretch his authority to anyone that God hadn't given him in his measure of rule. He knew he had authority to the Corinthians and in their church because of the work he had done to them and in them. He wasn't given authority in the work of others, knowing they had their own authority. He knew he was working with them and that God, would be able to bring them into the order they needed.

He knew that if he was established in the Corinthians, he would be able to go beyond them to the regions where the gospel wasn't preached yet. Then he wasn't encroaching on someone else's work, but on the work that God was doing through him. Knowing he didn't have supreme authority was quite a comfort to him and to those under his measure of rule. But that didn't diminish the amount of authority he had in the Corinthians. He might not have authority beyond them yet, but he had authority over them and it wasn't minor. He knew where he had authority and where he didn't and that made him an excellent leader.

In my own life, I have learned to understand where my authority lies and where it doesn't. Where I don't have authority, I submit to whomever has it. Where my authority does lie, I take it very seriously and with full accountability. When I am called to lead, I do it will full understanding that I will be held accountable before God for what happens. I am continually looking for those to submit to and to serve them the best I can while I am under their authority. If I have been given the authority, then I very seriously pray for wisdom and lead with all the grace and humility I can. I will make the hard decisions and stand by them. I will listen to those under me and receive input, but I am the one who will stand accountable for this and I will do it to the best of my ability. One of the greatest freedoms in the world is to know where your measure of rule is and to operate within those parameters. Where I don't have authority I can rest and relax and let others take the lead. I have to trust God to work in them all that is needed to accomplish His will. If they are having a problem and are really messing up, I submit to them and give what input I can to help, but the final decisions are theirs.

In a situation in Luke, Jesus encounters something that amazed Him. The subject was spiritual authority. Let's look at it.

Luke 7:2-10

And a certain slave of a centurion, one dear to him, having illness, was about to expire. And having heard about Jesus, he sent elders of the Jews to Him, asking Him that He might come to restore his slave. And coming to Jesus, they earnestly begged Him, saying, He to whom You give this is worthy. For he loves our nation, and he built the synagogue for us. And Jesus went with them. But He being yet not far away from the house, the centurion sent friends to Him, saying to Him, Lord, do not trouble, for I am not worthy that You come under my roof For this reason I did not count myself worthy to come to You. But say in a word, and let my servant be cured. For I also am a man having been set under authority, having soldiers under myself And I say to this one, Go! And he goes. And to another, Come! And he comes. And to my slave, Do this I And he does it. And hearing these things, Jesus marveled at him. And turning to the crowd following Him, He said, I say to you, I did not find such faith in Israel. And those sent, returning to the house, found the sick slave well.

What really got through to Jesus was the grasp the centurion had on authority. The centurion understood that when one had authority, he told those under him what to do and they did it. He told Jesus that he understood the authority Jesus had in the spirit realm that had effect in the physical realm. All Jesus had to do was to speak and all things would be done. That is amazing faith.

A few things in this passage stand out. The centurion had no other place to turn to. Nothing within his very considerable grasp was helping his servant. He knew someone had the ability to help. He heard about Jesus and went straight to the source. His money had no power here. But he did have friends and he used them to go to Jesus. Jesus was only sent to the last of Israel. He wasn't there for gentiles yet, but because of the influence of his friends and using this situation to show the hand of God, Jesus started to go to the centurion. They tried to cover all the bases as they told Jesus that the centurion was "worthy" because of what he had done for the Jewish community. This probably wasn't what swayed Him to go. The Father was showing Jesus what to do. Something here was important to the Father and Jesus followed.

While Jesus was still on the way, the centurion sent word not to come into the house. Going into a gentile home would make one unclean and the centurion knew this. He didn't want it to cost Jesus, instead he knew that Jesus could do it from a distance just as easily. He understood that this was an issue about authority. He knew Jesus had it.

I don't know how he knew this. This a very astute understanding that few have. There is spiritual authority that has rank over physical authority or even governmental authority. The centurion understood this somehow. He knew that in this area, the only one who had true authority was Jesus. He must have heard the stories of how Jesus healed and what He said. Since He commanded people to get up and walk or to see for the first time, He had authority in the realm of physical healing. Authority works over distance. There would be no problem to speak from where Jesus was and still be totally effective. He sent people to tell that to Jesus so that He didn't have to enter into his gentile home. He told Jesus to just speak it and it would happen. This caught Jesus by surprise. He wasn't expecting to encounter someone with this kind of faith.

It is faith that understands authority. He knew it would happen. He had complete faith that Jesus' words would work and heal his servant. Jesus had authority in the spiritual realm that was higher than the physical realm. His words had the power of creation in them. He could truly bless with power. All He had to do was to speak it into existence.

One of the greatest things the centurion understood was that to have authority you have to be submitted to it. He told Jesus that he is a man under authority and I say to this one go and he goes and to that one come and he comes. He didn't say that he had authority and things happened, but that he is under authority and things happen. Submission is the key to all authority. The more we submit, the more we are able to be trusted with the use of authority.

When in a situation, one must ask: who is in authority here? Where are my boundaries? Who should I submit to? Do I have any authority here? Is there someone I need to line up with to use my authority?

Learning about authority has been a life long journey for me. I wish I could say I have complete revelation about it, but I don't. It is more now than ever before, but it isn't total. Now I use authority in greater ways, though I don't always know in which situations to use it. When I do, things happen. When I don't have the authority in a certain area, my effectiveness is diminished.

We can learn much from the centurion. He knew where he had authority and where he didn't. He knew to seek those who did have it for there to be effectiveness. He knew how to submit and how to encourage those with authority to use it. And he did it all with boldness, not caring who knew what he knew or how limited he was. Jesus had some very good things to say about this gentile who had great faith. He said that those who knew religion didn't understand the things of the spirit like the centurion who knew about authority. May we all learn from this man.

An Area of Great Authority

When we are uncertain where we have authority and where we don't, we can turn to Scripture and see some of the areas where we were given the authority.

Luke 9:1

And having called together His twelve disciples, He gave them power and authority over all the demons, and to heal diseases.

Wow! This is a blanket authority along with the power (dunamis—ability to have a true effect). He sent them out two-by-two to minister and gave them power and authority. The first thing listed is over all demons. We still have authority over demons. Most have forgotten this or haven't received the revelation of it. When encountering demons most get into a shouting match thinking the louder they yell at the demon the greater they have authority over them. I have found the reverse to be true. The more authority I have, the less I have to yell. Simply speaking works quite well because along with my authority comes my faith. I know I am causing great pressure in the spirit realm. Demons don't argue with me anymore. They just leave.

It doesn't matter how big the demon is. Our authority is over *all* demons, even though they will try to lie to you and tell you differently. You have to have revelation about your authority. Then there will be no question and the demons leave.

When I help people discover how they let the demon in, then I usually have them cast it out with their authority, not mine. That helps them understand how to keep the demons out and they aren't bothered anymore. Out is out.

The problem arises when it comes to diseases. Some diseases go out quickly and others don't seem to be affected at all. It is a lifelong study in the realm of healing and how it all works. Since I am limited in scope in this book, the only thing I will discuss is that there are times, being directed by the Lord, that I have seen people use their authority and diseases leave. This is especially true in the area of curses. Once the curse is exposed, the blessing has greater authority. The curse is removed and the effect is immediate.

We have been working with people for a long time and have concluded that finding the root of the disease is the biggest key to healing. How did the disease come into their lives? Was it a curse?

Was it a lie they believed? Was it a sin they committed? Is there a judgment against someone, themselves, or God? Finding the root allows us to see what is needed and then the authority is applied. Then we see results most of the time. Sometimes there is no effect and people die or leave with their disease. If Jesus doesn't show us what to do and how, we are helpless. It is His ultimate authority that we are working with.

When dealing with healing, don't forget your authority. Are you submitted to those in authority? Are you humble and being a servant? Are you working with people to help them or are you just wanting to see healing? You have to love people first and foremost. Then the Lord can use you in many different areas of healing.

Luke 10:17-20

And the seventy returned with joy, saying, Lord, even the demons are subject to us through Your Name. And He said to them, I saw Satan falling out of Heaven as lightning! Behold, I have given you the authority to tread on snakes and scorpions, and on all the power of the hostile one, and nothing shall hurt you, no, never! But stop rejoicing in this, that the evil spirits submit to you. But rather rejoice that your names are written in Heaven.

What a statement! The disciples experienced how their authority worked in the spirit realm around them. They loved it! Jesus put them back in place by telling them what He had seen and why He had His authority. Then He told them that He had given them authority that caused effect around them. They could tread on snakes and scorpions without being hurt. They had authority over all the power of the enemy that really wanted to hurt them—the devil. But they had authority in such a way as to be safe from harm from the enemy! This is truly remarkable! I'm sure it was blowing their minds to think of all this in such a short period of time.

Then Jesus really steps it up. He said not to rejoice over the fact that evil spirits were subject to them, but rather that their names were written in Heaven. What a wonderful thing to understand. None of the vast ministries that we do are all that remarkable or praiseworthy. When God works, it is His works being done. None of us get the glory. The real praise is that we have salvation. We have life eternal and all of that because of grace. We didn't earn it or deserve it. It was offered. When we received our salvation, we received the Holy Spirit living within us. When we were baptized into the Holy Spirit, He came on us and empowered us for works outside ourselves. All that is done is for the praise of our God and Father and to bring Him the glory. When something happens in ministry, we must always remember that it isn't that we are so wonderful, but that He is so wonderful. I get the privilege to be used of God to help others. It is Him working through me that makes things happen. The more I realize this revelation, the more peace I have. All I have to do is be obedient.

The more I submit to Him, the more I am able to be used of Him. It is all about the authority I am submitted to and therefore able to use. Submission isn't a dirty word; it is the power of God to be able to bring all He does to others. He uses all the forms of authority to bring me to the place I need to be, to do what He wants me to do.

Summary

This whole discussion brings me full circle to where we started. It is how we view ourselves that makes submission easy or difficult. If I am a slave, then I have no rights and no self-promotion. The more I see myself as one to serve others, the more the Father can trust me to use His giftings and anointings. The more I promote myself, the more I taint all that He gives me. If I can be set free from all the hurts and lies I believe, then I can be a usable vessel to bring all He has to others. God opposes the proud and gives grace to the humble. I get to choose who I want to be. As long as I am trying to get others to give me what I need, I won't be trusting Him to help me find the things I need. Trusting myself or others is a curse. Trusting Him is blessed. I need to lay down my soul to love others and to serve them without trying to get something back from them. I must forgive and not judge. I must not be able to be offended. I must help a brother that is in sin. I must be a good friend.

All the aspects of relationship are mostly covered in one thing: submission. Humbling ourselves is the key to all of it. The more we submit, the more God can touch us and heal us. Then we are able to touch others the way He needs us to.

The only relationship we really need to have is the one with Jesus on a personal, minute-by-minute basis. No religion, only relationship. Knowing Him, loving Him, talking to Him, hearing from Him, submitting to Him, and obeying Him is what is important and will meet all the needs of our souls. As we know Him and His love for people, then we will gain how He sees them. Only then can we have the relationships He has called us to have.

May God richly bless us as we endeavor to find Him and His relationship with others.

ABOUT THE AUTHOR

Lee Eddy is a Bible teacher and seminar speaker who has developed several ministries to help people become who they are in Christ. He has developed and employed a one-on-one healing ministry dealing with deep wounds, personal needs, addictions, and marriages. He lives in Denver, Colorado with his wife of over forty years. They have three children and two grandchildren.

CPSIA information can be obtained
at www.ICGtesting.com
Printed in the USA
FFOW02n1616180418
46262208-47689FF